TEN YEARS TO MOTHERHOOD

From Tragedy to Triumph

A Journey of Faith Grown
In the Wilderness

Megan Angus-Hylton

Please note that pseudo-names are used for some persons in this account.

For Workshops, Conferences, Webinars, Counselling & Coaching Sessions, contact Megan Hylton.

Email: meganhylton91@gmail.com

Tel./WhatsApp: 876-524-6437

Facebook: Oasis Counselling & Coaching Services

Edited by: Yetunda McLean Dixon

Cover Design: HCP Book Publishing

Published by HCP Book Publishing

ENDORSEMENTS

"I wholeheartedly endorse Megan Angus-Hylton's book, 'Ten Years to Motherhood'. Having ministered to Megan during her journey, I witnessed her faith and resilience as she navigated the challenges of infertility. Her story is a testament to God's faithfulness and redemption, offering hope and inspiration to those facing similar struggles. I am honoured to recommend this book, which chronicles her journey from struggle to triumph, culminating in the joy of motherhood."

Bishop Dr. Roderick Senior
Administrative Bishop
COGOP: St. Catherine West

****

"I have had the privilege of hearing Minister Megan Hylton's remarkable testimony, and it's truly one of the most faith-filled stories I have ever encountered. Listening to her story has been a powerful injection of faith into my own heart, inspiring me to trust God for children of my own. Every book she has written has had a profound impact, and I have no doubt that her latest work will be just as life changing. It is a testament to the transformative power of faith and prayer, which can produce miracles in our lives."

Rev. Kimola Brown-Lowe
Campus Pastor-WAFIF Florida

****

"This is the book you've been waiting for. Megan did not sugar-coat her experience. You will feel validated. Finally, someone understands. Finally, someone has put words to the pain and longing. But she doesn't end it there. The wrestling within her to contend with her reality of childlessness and still hold that burning desire to become a mother is evident. Hope is woven through every chapter of this book. Whether it's from her thoughts, a reminder of a word from God or a scripture that the Lord keeps bringing her to. Your faith will be ignited. Buy this book. Read this book and be encouraged."

Tamaya Wilson
Counselling Psychologist

****

"Becoming a mother is a true blessing from God. Megan has always had a strong faith in God and he has delivered on his promises to her. I am truly happy to have walked the journey with her and delivered her three beautiful daughters. She is a wonderful woman of God and a great mother to her three daughters. I pray God's continued blessings on her entire family as she continues to inspire and uplift others on this journey of motherhood. This book will undoubtedly bring inspiration, faith and hope to many."

Dr. Sharmaine Mitchell
Consultant Gynaecologist & Obstetrician

****

"In Ten Years to Motherhood, Mrs. Megan Hylton offers a deeply honest and courageous account of a journey many women walk in silence. Her vulnerability gives voice to the longing, disappointment, hope, and faith that accompany delayed motherhood. This book is not just a story - it is a companion for women who have wrestled with waiting, uncertainty, and unanswered prayers. Mrs. Hylton reminds us that even in the delay, purpose is being formed. A powerful, compassionate read for every woman who has ever wondered if her time would come."

Dawn-Marie Smith
Counselling Psychologist

****

"Megan Hyton's journey toward motherhood spans a decade marked by faith, perseverance, and countless encounters that capture the essence of waiting and trusting God - the One who holds every answer. Her story stands as a powerful reminder that He who began a good work is faithful to complete it and that God watches over His word to fulfill it.

Ten Years to Motherhood: From Tragedy to Triumph - A Journey of Faith Grown in the Wilderness beautifully illustrates what unfolds when faith and hope lead the way to a testimony of victory.

If you are in a season of waiting for a precious gift while navigating your own valley moments, this book is for you. It offers practical tools to strengthen your faith as you wait and reminds you that your story is not over. Happy reading."

Minister Tanesha Johnson

FOREWORD

To the glory of Almighty God, we lift high, the name of Jesus and commend this work as a living testimony of the Dunamis power of the Holy Ghost operating in the life of the believer.

This book is a prophetic declaration and a faith-filled chronicle of God's miraculous intervention in the life of Minister Hylton. Each chapter resounds the reality of process and the wind of the Spirit that carries barren seasons into fruitful destinies. It speaks to the valleys of waiting and the mountains of hope, reminding readers that delay does not invalidate God's will for your life, and that the promises of God are indeed, yes and amen.

Minister Hylton releases the strength to hold fast to your vision! Do not allow the enemy's lies or the weight of reality to abort what you know the Word of God says about your life. This is a book for those who may feel discouraged, who need to lift their faith, and those standing in the gap for others. It is also for every believer who dares to believe that the same God who opened Sarah's womb to deliver a child, is still performing wonders today.

We bless our daughter, Minister Megan Angus-Hylton, for her obedience and travail in birthing this message of hope and sharing her testimony. We decree and declare that this manuscript will ignite faith, stir expectation, and usher many into their season of manifestation. To every married couple seeking breakthrough, anchor your soul in the sovereignty of God. As He did for the Hyltons, He will do it for you, for His glory and by His Spirit! May the grace of conception to delivery be your portion in Jesus Name.

Blessings in Christ,

Apostle Dr. Courtney McLean
Reverend Nadine McLean
Senior Pastors
Worship and Faith International Fellowship

ACKNOWLEDGMENTS

Thanks be to God who always causes me to triumph in Christ Jesus. I thank God for His enabling grace to put into words a journey that I know was pregnant with purpose.

Thanks to my husband, Winston. I would choose no one else to walk this journey with. To my wonderful miracle children thank you for believing in this vision and cheering me on from start to finish.

Heartfelt gratitude to my spiritual parents Apostle Dr. Courtney McLean and Rev. Nadine McLean, your Spirit-led teachings have brought much clarity and wisdom to what I walked through. I am now ready to share my story with the world for the glory of God. Thank you for praying for and motivating me to persevere and produce this work that God placed in my heart.

Special thanks to my publisher, Mr. Cleveland McLeish and to Dr. Taj-Marie Hunter, Mrs. Yetunda Dixon and Dr. Kenroy Waldo for your assistance in helping to bring this dream to reality.

DEDICATION

I dedicate this book to God who chose me to carry a mega testimony - my story is for His glory. I dedicate this work also to my amazing children who God used to create a beautiful narrative of how powerful God is. You deserve to know the journey and just how special you are to me.

I write this book for the many women who have suffered the disappointment of barrenness, the excruciating pain of a miscarriage or the numbing trauma of stillbirth. I write for the men who struggle to stand through the pain of losing an unborn child or who face the chilling monster of infertility. I write to bring encouragement, healing and hope and to point you to the One who walked me through a very difficult season of my life-one moment at a time.

I write this book for the person who has received a promise from God but feels forgotten in the wilderness called waiting. May you receive a faith injection as you turn the pages of this book and may you be reminded that despite what you are seeing now - Jehovah has the final say!

A WORD FROM THE AUTHOR

The things that are unseen are just as real and probably more real than the things that are seen. I have learned over time that God often teaches spiritual lessons through physical experiences. This book is a recollection of my personal journey dealing with infertility a physical experience through which I learned many spiritual and life lessons.

It was a rough season but one filled with purpose and divine destiny created to build within me an unwavering faith that developed through the wilderness of waiting. I invite you to relive that journey with me with the hope that you will be healed and lifted in your faith in God and that every barren area in your life will bear fruit and manifest TRUTH.

I write this book as a testimonial of the miracle working power of God; a testimony that He is God and He cannot lie. I write in response to a prophetic word received while still in the process, that what I was going through was not about me, it was for those God would use my story to encourage. I write this account as the fulfilment of a promise I made to God in 2008 on a hospital bed, "If you give me the desire of my heart and change my story, I will testify!"

Receive this testimony for the glory of God.

Contents

INTRODUCTION

What do you do when you find yourself facing the same disappointment over and over again? How do you continue to believe for the impossible when everything before your eyes confirms the impossibility of what you are hoping for? For several years, each New Year's Day though a joy for many, was a cold reminder to me of another year lost, another year of shattered hope -my womb still empty and silent. For ten years, my life felt like a roller-coaster ride of hope and grief. Life had become a wilderness of doctor's appointments, bad medical reports, dashed dreams and hidden tears. By God's grace, I managed to build a career, a home, a life and a ministry to teens that seemed fulfilling on the outside, but deep inside, my soul ached with emptiness. The doctors told me to accept my fate but something in my heart refused to surrender, telling me to increase my faith.

This book is the story of that decade long battle-the raw, unfiltered account of my journey through the valleys of tragedy and despair that can accompany infertility. It is about me learning to lean on a faith that was sometimes fragile but that would over time become the firm foundation for my greatest triumph.

More than just an account, this is a testament that even in our darkest seasons, faith can grow and produce a miraculous future that eventually becomes a present reality we never imagined possible.

The wilderness is often seen as a place of barrenness and lack but the wilderness can also be a place of revelation, divine encounters with God and deep transformation and growth. Treasures can be gleaned from a wilderness experience. It is a place pregnant with purpose and packed with potential.

Many persons I believe, expected this to have been my first book, but God is intentional. There are things I needed to further process and understand as I was fathered spiritually on another level. The time is now. The lessons from the journey are clear. The treasures from the wilderness are now made plain to me. May lives be touched for the glory of God as I recount my journey to steadfast faith.

If you have ever felt forgotten, disappointed and broken by life; trapped in a wilderness of waiting, this book is for you. May hope arise within your heart as I reflect on my experiences and the lessons learned enroute to motherhood.

May you be inspired to dream again, believe again, declare again; and may God grant you the intricate desires of your heart. Welcome to my journey.

Chapter I

THE DREAM CONCEIVED

"**L**adies and gentlemen, please stand and welcome for the first time, Mr. & Mrs. Hylton!" The wedding guests erupted with excitement, echoing the joy we felt in our hearts, an unshakeable sense that God was weaving our lives into a story far bigger than ourselves.

At just 21 years old, I found true love. We both believed that we were meant to journey through life together. We prayed earnestly and sought wise counsel. Though some persons believed that we were still too young for marriage, the blessings of those closest to our hearts and the peace of God strengthened our resolve. And so, on a bright Jamaican Saturday morning in June 1999, we exchanged vows and became husband and wife. The future looked bright with promise; our hearts were filled with anticipation for the years that lay ahead.

Our first home was the smaller side of a large house. A couple who were long-time friends of ours occupied the larger section of the building. Three weeks after our marriage their beautiful baby girl, CeeCee, was born. We were very fond of CeeCee and she eventually became like our own. Her mother was quite nervous to carry out certain tasks with her newborn, but I found delight in doing them. I had garnered some experience from taking care of my younger cousins while living with my aunt during my teenaged years.

By the time CeeCee reached eight months old, she had already developed a strong sense of curiosity and independence. Each morning, after she was fed, she would make her way across the verandah, crawling eagerly towards our side of the house and knocking her little hands on the door for us to let her in. Interacting with her daily sparked within me the desire to become a mother. She made me feel like I was born for motherhood and ready for it. On the contrary, we were advised repeatedly by well-meaning persons, "No babies within the first year! Take the time to get to know each other well." We took their advice, so the thought of starting a family early never crossed our minds. Having a child—at least within that first year—simply was not a part of our plan.

Eventually, I began to wonder if delaying was really a good idea or if we should just let nature take its course. After all, we were married! I didn't give much thought to the desire I was having because I really believed that we needed to lay a strong foundation as a newly married couple before bringing a child into the picture. I was not worried at all. I was convinced that I would easily become a mother whenever we were ready. For now, helping with CeeCee was enough and it was good practice too.

In 2000, CeeCee's parents began to build their own home in a distant community, and I knew the inevitable was coming-they would be moving away. As the day drew closer, I tried to comfort myself with the thought that I would still see her at church and could visit their home as well.

About a week before they moved out I started feeling ill. I was queasy most of the day and very, very sleepy. 'Could it be that I was pregnant? Naaaa. I don't think so,' I thought. I managed to convince myself that I had probably eaten something that was affecting me in some way. One evening, Winston and I took a ride to the country with a friend. On our way back I started having terrible abdominal cramps. I said nothing to anyone as I figured it was just regular cramps, nothing to be alarmed about. The pain grew progressively worse throughout the night to the point where my anguish could no longer be hidden.

The next morning, Winston took me to see a gynaecologist in Kingston. After routine checks and reviewing my symptoms, he commented, "Mr. and Mrs. Hylton, I am afraid you might be having a miscarriage."

In that moment I felt like I was in a dream, "A what?!"

The doctor slowly explained that he believed I had been about 6 to 8 weeks pregnant but I was losing the baby. I was in shock. He informed that he would allow my body to carry through the process naturally and I should return the next day for an ultrasound. The drive home that day was long and awkward. Winston spoke occasionally trying to ensure that I was okay. I was in a space that is even now difficult to describe.

The ultrasound the following day proved Dr. Michaels right. I had lost a baby. He tried to encourage me stating that these things 'happen' and that he saw no reason why I would not conceive again soon. I am not sure now that I heard even half of what he was saying. I felt numb. Winston and I held hands and prayed that night, asking God for strength, hope, healing and peace. He is our very present help in times of trouble (Psalm 46:1).

The next few days were difficult for us. We told very close relatives (probably not a good idea now that I think about it). They tried to encourage us but not all were successful. I remember one person explaining that God was testing me to see if I was ready and I obviously was not, so he took the child. Seriously?! Hmmm. That hurt deeply but I did not have the strength at the time to respond. I let it be, not knowing that the enemy would use those words to haunt me for years to come. I now know that as a Christian you must address some things immediately because words are seeds and some seeds must be destroyed before they take root and grow.

As I grieved silently, I found peace from the presence of God. Worship became my place of safety. I knew He was with me in this life moment and that was reassuring. I also found some solace in Dr. Michaels' comments that I would probably conceive again soon. The fact that I got pregnant meant that there was hope for it to happen again. There began my dream of being a mother and eventually, an obsession with getting pregnant. Sounds negative, right? Well, maybe it was to some degree but it was that hunger that would help to fuel my faith to push against all the odds that I was about to face.

I was still recovering from having lost the child I never knew about but over time my desire to have a child grew stronger. God often uses our negative experiences to spark a fire towards what we must ultimately become. In the account of Joseph's life in the book of Genesis, Chapters 37-41, we see where Joseph was destined for greatness; favoured by his father, envied by his brothers and motherless. Amid the familial chaos, God was giving Joseph dreams-dreams that pointed to who he would become and what his destiny was in the mind of God. Dreams that seemed like arrogant imaginations to his family members, were pregnant with prophetic imagery and meaning and Joseph could not deny what God was depositing in his heart. I felt something inside my heart that I could not deny. I felt like I was born for motherhood and the desire was steadily increasing.

Wilderness Treasures:

1. **God sits with us in every season.** Being in God's will does not exempt us from difficult experiences but he promises to be with us in and through life's storms.

2. **Amid pain, God can deposit a dream in your heart that contradicts your current situation.** That dream conceived can produce life-changing faith.

3. **Do not allow negative words to go unaddressed.** If you cannot address them publicly, address them in prayer. Words are seeds and some word seeds must not be allowed to live.

Despite my loss, I felt hope, a dream inside me of holding my own child and nothing I tried seemed to quell it! God had sown the seed through the feeling I had when I held CeeCee and through the words of Dr. Michaels. Pain and disappointment had come my way, but God continued to water the dream. I kept hearing the thought, 'if it happened once, it can happen again'. I couldn't help but think about it, feel it, imagine it and mentally prepare for it. The dream had been conceived.

Chapter 2

REALITY CHECK

CAUGHT IN A CYCLE

The dream was conceived and I was hopeful that it was close to manifestation but the approaching months and years would confront me with harsh realities that would challenge everything I believed.

What is reality? The Oxford Dictionary defines reality as the state of things as they actually exist. Many times, as believers our reality does not match the dream or vision that God has placed in our hearts. The greater the discrepancy - the greater the challenge. How we handle these contradictions on our journey to faith depends greatly on our spiritual maturity at that particular time.

The month immediately following the first miscarriage in 2001, I again had symptoms of pregnancy. Anxiously but without telling my husband I did a pregnancy test. It was positive but somewhat pale. I chose not to say anything to him that day. About three days later I woke up in excruciating abdominal cramps. "No! Not again!" I thought. This time I broke emotionally. The pain in my heart was more than I could handle. I cried in anger and disappointment... this was totally crazy! It didn't fit the script at all! I cried alone at home for close to two hours. It was just too much.

At a place of pain, we may speak rashly - this strongly depends on how spiritually mature and secure we are. I had been saved for ten years and was very involved in church activities but was I secure in who I was in the eyes of the Lord? No. So as I cried that day, I said out loud what I felt inside: *"What have I done wrong? Why did I have to go through this? Is this how you pay me for trying to please you?"* I later asked for forgiveness just in case in my anger I had charged God foolishly. Job 1 vs. 22 (KJV) states: 'In all this, Job sinned not nor charged God foolishly.' The Amplified Version of the Bible puts it this way: 'Through all this, Job did not sin, nor did he blame God.' May God grant you the same grace that even when your reality hits hard you will not sin and you will not blame God or charge him foolishly.

Two days later I was back at the Dr. Michaels' office. This time, I got a different explanation, "Mrs Hylton, I don't think you were pregnant this time around. This may have been what we call a chemical pregnancy. Your body produced the hormone, but you really were not pregnant."

He further explained that maybe I had residual pregnancy hormones from the previous failed pregnancy which could have also caused the positive test result. Okay then-so this was a false alarm? Hmmm.

Deep inside, I didn't like where this was going. I began reading about pregnancies—the signs, symptoms, risks, etc. CeeCee's mom was convinced she was having no other child, so she gave me a book she had about pregnancy and childbirth. I read sections of it every day. I also bought other books-very expensive health books on pregnancy. One day while at work at the Point Hill Primary and Junior High School, a co-worker brought a book to work so she could use it in a science class. That book was phenomenal, it explained everything about conception, pregnancy and childbirth simply. Whenever I had some free sessions, I would borrow her book and read, read, read. Slowly but surely, I was becoming consumed with the desire to become pregnant. Each month I would 'feel' pregnant, then I would face the disappointment of another menstrual period, but before the end of the period I would convince myself that I was pregnant and the period was just slight bleeding from the baby attaching himself to the womb. This I had learned from my reading.

Obsession, even about a good thing can open the door to oppression. Eventually, I found myself in a vicious cycle that was emotionally exhausting for both my husband and me. When you carry a God-given dream, the devil will try to contaminate that dream and frustrate you into letting go of your faith. Eventually, I stopped seeing myself properly. My self-image was deteriorating rapidly. I no longer felt like that potential mother but more like a perpetual failure. Each month as the physical and mental cycle continued, my self-esteem plummeted more and more. Yet I kept searching for answers. I spoke with those persons I trusted most, seeking affirmation, encouragement and hope.

BAD PROGNOSIS

One of my sisters-in-law eventually recommended a gynaecologist to me and I went for my first visit, hoping he would have some good news for me. He was very thorough I must admit. What followed that initial visit was months of tests, bad reports and further anxieties and some rather humiliating moments. We did blood tests, sperm count tests, fallopian tube tests. The thoughts alone are wearisome so imagine living that reality.

From the results received, Dr. Wallace delivered the news that we were clinically infertile. Both of us had extremely low levels of specific hormones making it basically impossible for me to get pregnant. The thought of living my life in the shadow of other women who were mothers was debilitating. My husband was being affected by this too as the questions were shooting at us from all angles. Friends, relatives, church members and acquaintances asked, "When is the baby coming? We've waited long enough!"

My reality was a major contradiction to the dream I carried in my heart. It was a confusing place for me. Was I to reject my dream and embrace what medical science was saying? I had no evidence for the dream but the test results were clear.

Dr. Wallace encouraged me saying that maybe one day my body would surprise me. I left his office that day feeling like I had lost another major battle; but in the darkness of disappointment there still flickered a candle of hope that God would not allow to go out. Somehow, I still believed-at least a little.

Within a year I was at another doctor who I will call Dr. Tate. He had been recommended by a friend. Again, we were instructed to do various tests which we did. At about 11 p.m. one night, my cell phone rang. Dr Tate called to inform me that he received the test results and that they did not look good. Both our hormonal levels were so low that his only recommendation for us was adoption.

As we ended the call, I knew in my heart that that was our final conversation. His language and mindset were not what I needed to hear at that time. Some may argue that I was in denial and from a psychological perspective it certainly looked that way; but his recommendation did not match what I felt and what I was praying for. I cannot blame him though; he was speaking as a doctor based on the scientific results he had before him. I put my phone down and decided not to tell my husband about that call until many years later. What he needed to hear was hope not hopelessness.

My emotions intensified at this stage of the journey. Journalling gives you the opportunity to write your story while living it. I found it difficult to express what I was feeling to those around me– I kept most of what I knew to myself, and my journal became my safe place:

How I Feel and What I Think

My life is somewhat okay. I have a lot to be thankful for but there's one area that is just constantly there to bother me. At age 22 I got married very excited about the future and knowing that I truly loved my husband. We made such a wonderful couple. I'd always loved children but that was not at the front of my mind as I embarked on this leg of my journey through life, maybe because it was a given – we would have children no doubt about that – just not immediately after marriage.

Ten months later I was told that I was six weeks (approximately) pregnant but lost it the next day. Since that time 7 years ago, I've been a different person. My whole life has centered on becoming a mother. I've been to doctors, done tests, taken tablets, prayed and fasted, used the word, believed God, bought baby clothes and other items, received baby gifts, chosen name and **NOTHING**.

Am I angry? Yes! Am I disappointed? Yes!

I'm angry and disappointed. I'm angry because I cannot see a logical reason behind all of this. I don't think it's fair to me to have to go through this turmoil. I became a Christian as a teenager and I promised myself and God that I would not have sex until I was married. I kept that promise even though I had opportunities to do otherwise, I never had sex until the night of my wedding in 1999. Of course this was not because I am more saved than anyone else it was God's grace working for me but if I had not made the decision I would have fallen. Knowing that I obeyed his word and wanted until marriage, I just took it for granted that God would ensure that everything went okay for me where fertility and reproductive health are concerned. Instead, this is what I get.

I'm angry because what I'm experiencing contradicts the word of God which says "No good thing will be withheld from those that walk uprightly. God alone knows how much this means to me yet every month I face the same disappointment. I expected God to ensure that the man I marry and me were able to produce children. He is God and I can't tell Him what to do but that's how I feel.

Sometimes I feel less than a woman especially when I see my peers with their children and the joys that's on their faces and I wonder how it feels and why I have been deprived of it. I feel like I've been punished for a sin I'm unaware of. At times I honestly believe that if I had sex with my husband before the wedding, we would be parents now and it makes me wonder if it was really worth it to not have had sex before.

I have thought of adoption but deep down that's not what I want. I want to get pregnant, give birth and watch my children grow. If God didn't intend for me to have children He would not place this intense feeling inside me. I have an area of emptiness inside of me that I believe having a child will fill.

I have prayed asking God to forgive me if this thing has become an idol but I've tried and the desire won't go away. I have almost buried myself in church work to try to forget it but it's still there. I am sick of feeling this way. Even those who used to encourage me to have faith are avoiding talking to me now. I guess they don't know what else to say.

A part of me is afraid that this is it - that things won't change. But a greater part can't help but believe that God will not leave me comfortless. He has spoken to my heart so many times that it's hard for me not to expect Him to work.

Nobody knows that I feel these things because I recognise that everyone expects me to be strong and have faith so over the years, I've learned not to show my pain. I show it to God in our private times but recently I hardly even talk to Him much about it because He already knows.

I guess I have no choice but to try to keep my head above the water and live my life and accomplish my other dreams because this is one I can't MAKE happen. Only God can do that. I've tried, really tried and nothing works. All I know, I know how Elizabeth must have felt and it's not a nice feeling. But like Elizabeth, may God visit me and change my story.

Wilderness Treasures:

1. **Your calling and anointing do not exempt you from pain.**

It often positions you for it. Spiritual resilience and tenacity are often developed in the place of pain. When obstacles and challenges come your way-as unbearable as it may feel, remember the reality you are facing might just be a part of the process of your making. God often uses situations in our lives -to build our character, increase our faith and transform us into His image. *The true soldier is trained at the base and in the barracks but he is made on the battlefield.* Trust God during your making season. James encouraged the believers to see the testing of their faith in a positive light because it produces patience. It's a journey of becoming; a journey of transformation, a journey of faith developed in the wilderness.

2. **After the dream is conceived, it will be tested.**

In Genesis Chapters 37-50 we read the account of Joseph's life. Joseph moved from having powerful dreams about a prosperous future to being thrown into a pit- left to die then sold into slavery by his own brothers! His reality initially did not match his dreams, but he did not lose faith. I challenge you today, remember that the presence of opposing realities in your life does not equate to the absence of God's purpose in your life. Before it manifests, the word or promise of God often tries the one to whom it was sent, (Psalm 105 vs. 17-19). If the promise was indeed sent by God, it will not return to him void or barren; it MUST prosper in the thing to which it was sent. Isaiah 55 vs. 11: *"So shall My word be that goeth forth out of My mouth: It shall not return unto me void, but it shall accomplish that which I please, and it shall prosper in the thing whereto I sent it."* May every word

God has deposited in you prosper in you and return unto him bearing fruit!

3.   Your current reality should not kill your dream.

What is the reality that you are facing that is defying the validity of your God-given dream? Isaiah asked the question of Israel in Isaiah 53 vs. 1 *"Who hath believed our report and to whom is the arm of the Lord revealed?"* I ask you today, daughter of God, son of God: Whose report will you believe? The arm (help, strength) of the Lord will be revealed to those who believe the report that comes from Him. As a legitimate child your Heavenly Father is always present with you. Even when it appears as if He is nowhere near to you, He is there. He takes covenant seriously and He promised to be with you ALWAYS. Do not allow your reality to silence the promise of God that fuels and energizes you on your journey of faith.

May the arm of the Lord be evident in your life as you choose to believe all that he has spoken over you.

My reality was painful, but it was a necessary part of the story God was composing through my life. I could not change reality but I could seek to manage how it affected me. The same is true for you. You may not be able to change the reality around you but believe me you have the power to decide how it will affect you. The great Titanic ship was built to master the seas and that it did until the sea got inside it. Be intentional to guard what gets inside you.

Chapter 3

THE BATTLE OF REALITY VS. TRUTH

After receiving several medical reports and consistent feedback from my doctors, I became depressed. I wore depression like a cloak and sunk beneath it daily like a secure place of hiding. Occasionally, I would 'come up for air', usually during that one week every month when I was 'convinced' that I was pregnant. When the reality hit that it was not so, I would break again emotionally. My mind was constantly bombarded with the burden of my situation. It felt like I was stuck in a recurring nightmare and could not wake from it. The enemy's plan was to kill my faith and ultimately abort my destiny. How was I preserved through all of this? The Word of God is truly the sword of the Spirit. Several verses were used by God to provide hope and peace to my heart. His truth was used to confront my reality.

According to the Mirriam-Webster Dictionary, truth is the real facts about something; that which is true. For the believer, truth refers to that which God has said about a situation, or whatever God has pre-destined for you even if it has not yet been revealed to you. In many instances our 'reality' is in stark contrast to God's truth about us and we may experience an inner battle between what we see happening (Reality) and what God has spoken (Truth).

The Bible gives several accounts of men and women of God who faced similar battles between their reality and God's truth. Joseph's reality was that he was sold by his brothers as a slave in a strange land but according to God's truth he was the Prime Minister of Egypt. At one point in his life, Moses' reality was being a fugitive tending sheep in the desert, but the divine truth was that he was the Israelite chosen by God to deliver His people from slavery. Peter's reality was that after three and a half years walking with Jesus, He denied him publicly three times, but God's truth about him was that he was the Apostle Peter, who would carry the Gospel of Jesus to nations. David was the youngest son of Zebedee, often left just to care for the sheep but God's truth identified him as the next King of Israel, a man after God's own heart. Megan Hylton was childless and diagnosed barren (reality), but God said she would bear children (truth)!

FAITH BOOSTER SCRIPTURES AND MOMENTS

Something profound happens when God adds His voice to your story. God's truth in your life, always produces change if it is received wholeheartedly. What proceeds from the mouth of God to you or from the heart of God about you, is the truth that can confront and conquer any opposing reality. God found ways to inject His truth into my spirit when my present reality was choking faith out of me. In John 8 vs. 32, Jesus declared, "And you shall know the truth and the truth will make you free."

My encounters with the truth of God through the scriptures served as faith boosters. In the field of agriculture, farmers sometimes use boosters to stimulate growth, add nutrients and provide extra-vitamins to plants and seeds. Boosters are substances that come with various benefits including enhancing plant resilience to drought and improving nutrient and water intake.

The faith boosters from the Word that God would reveal to me on my journey nurtured the seed of faith that was sown in my heart - my dream to become a mother. They helped to protect the seed as it grew in the soil of my heart threatened by negative thoughts and the drought of depression, fear and hopelessness that my reality was hurling at me. The scriptures below were essential in sustaining my spirit and building resilience in me when my reality felt overwhelming. They served as reminders that at any moment, God could change my story. Many of them are highlighted and dated in my Bible because God spoke to me through them when I needed to hear him most -faith boosters.

Faith Booster 1:

Isaiah 54: 1 "Sing O barren woman you who have never borne a child burst into song!"

Repeatedly, God would allow me to see this verse. It was a constant challenge for me to rejoice even when my story seemed like it was not changing.   It reminded me of the power God had to change my story drastically.

Faith Booster 2:

The Story of Hannah-1 Samuel 1-3

Hannah desired a child and for years she faced ridicule and torment. Her rival Peninah was loud and intrusive. Hannah continued to honour God and offer the required sacrifices to Him even through her pain. She poured her heart out to God and through his servant, Eli, the priest, a declaration was released into the atmosphere and over her life. Her request was granted. Eli uttered divine truth in the glaring face of a dark reality. Hannah chose to grab on to truth, and she brought forth a prophet (Samuel) and gave him to the Lord's service as she had promised. As you wait, whose report will you believe? What will you hold on to? Your reality or the truth of God?

I saw myself in the pages of Hannah's story, my Peninahs were subtle but many. They asked questions and made cynical remarks, sometimes casting a verdict that obviously I would never be a mother. Like Hannah, there were days when I questioned God, I questioned my husband, I questioned my faith, and yes like Hannah there were days when I cried uncontrollably before God in prayer, to the point where my tears became my words.

Hannah's story was used repeatedly by God to remind me that He had the final say. On one occasion, one of my then mentors saw me and smiled and said, "Hannah how are you?" Wow! That sounded like when Eli spoke to Hannah and gave her hope. I felt hope that day. The truth of God had again confronted my reality.

Faith Booster 3:

Psalm 3. The Lifter of my Head.

"LORD, how many are my foes! How many rise up against me! Many are saying of me, 'God will not deliver him.' But you, LORD, are a shield around me, my glory, the One who lifts my head high. I call out to the LORD, and He answers me from His holy mountain. I lie down and sleep; I wake again, because the LORD sustains me. I will not fear though tens of thousands assail me on every side. Arise, LORD! Deliver me, my God! Strike all my enemies on the jaw; break the teeth of

the wicked. From the LORD comes deliverance. May your blessing be on your people."

This psalm is dear to me because even in my seasons of depression, each time I heard the song written from this psalm, it lifted my spirit. The spirit of a man or woman who is connected to God will always respond to the voice of God. Even when I wanted to resist in the face of my reality, my heart was responding to the truth in that psalm - 'God is my glory and the lifter up of my head.'

A profound incident associated with this psalm, also happened about 5 years into waiting. I visited a church one Sunday morning. I literally wanted to be in a space where no one really knew me. My husband was in no mood to leave home so I told him I had to go on my own because I needed to be in a certain atmosphere as I felt emotionally low. I arrived at this church, my mentor who had called me Hannah was the pastor there but not many persons knew me. I found a cozy seat towards the back and sat expecting nothing really but just knowing I needed to be there that day. Their worship sessions were always rich with the presence of God and I needed that. I was disappointed when I realized my mentor was not the preacher that morning. The guest preacher, a man I had never seen before, Pastor Dick, took his place at the podium. After doing the usual greetings, he said, "God gave me a word for someone here today." My depressed mind responded sarcastically, "Lucky for them."

Pastor Dick asked all visitors in the congregation to stand. I obeyed and was quite happy to see that I was not the only one standing. He welcomed us then continued, "If you are standing and you are a teacher, keep standing. Everyone else can take your seats."

I looked around quickly and only two of us were left standing! I wanted to vanish but there was nowhere to disappear to. The preacher then spoke directly to me, using Psalm 3. He said, "God said to tell you that He is your glory and the lifter up of your head. He said stop walking with your head down. Your shame is coming to an end because He will lift your head!"

What do you do when the eternal God confronts the lies of the enemy with his Rhema word of truth? Receive and believe truth over reality. Truth always wins! As that prophetic word was released, I felt like my Heavenly Father used His hand and gently raised my chin-lifting my head in the realm of the Spirit. An injection of faith and hope had been administered to me.

I went home assured that I was not forgotten. My head would be lifted. What an assurance-God is good! No matter where you are on your journey to faith, make a decision to allow your steps to be led by God. My desire to visit that church that day was orchestrated by the Spirit of God because He knew He had sent a word there for me that day. Be careful not to miss God because you are led only by your intellect or your emotions and not by the promptings of the Holy Spirit.

Faith Booster 4:

Abraham's Long Wait-Genesis 12-21

God's Promise to Abraham: He would be the father of nations.
Abraham's Reality: Sarah, Abraham's wife was barren.

According to Genesis Chapter 12, Abraham left his kindred and country, in obedience to God's instructions, to go to 'a place' and the promise he got while on his way to that place was that he would become the father of nations. His reality though was barrenness in bold capital letters. His wife, Sarah was barren and she was barren for a very, very long time.

Abraham's story is a testament of what it means to believe God and to wait on God in faith. I read Abraham's story numerous times while I waited for my story to change. There were several things about his life that encouraged and also intrigued me.

- ***Truth eventually wins over reality.***

At no point did God ever change his mind about Abraham becoming the father of nations. At intervals, He would remind Abraham of His promise to him especially when his reality was a contradiction to the promise. The truth of God was not cancelled by the delay Abraham and Sarah experienced. Once God utters a promise, it is established. Isaiah 14 vs. 27 declares, ***"For the Lord of hosts has decided and planned, <u>and</u> who can annul it?"*** (AMP).

- ***Abraham spoke with God from his heart.***

How safe are you emotionally with your Heavenly Father. When you pray do you really bear your heart before Him? I believe that one of the reasons why Abraham was called "the friend of God" is because he was willing to speak with God truthfully from his heart (see 2 Chronicles 20:7). Intimacy with God develops in the soul and spirit of men when we are open and vulnerable with Him. Intimacy grows in the place of nakedness. A couple cannot truly experience the heights of intimacy fully clothed. As Abraham was open with God, God revealed more and drew closer to him.

- ***Abraham walked in obedience.***

Even when his reality seemed to portray God as a liar, Abraham obeyed God. He never played hard-ball or tried to blackmail or bargain with God about the promise. He never withdrew his obedience even when the delay looked like denial. '

- ***Abraham was a worshipper.***

Many times, his worship flowed from his experiences with God and sometimes from a place of brokenness. In those times of worship God would often remind him of the promise. When you feel broken, translate that brokenness into worship. Authentic worship from a place of pain carries an aroma that God will not ignore.

- ***Abraham became temporarily distracted by the discomfort of Sarah.***

Sometimes it's hard to encourage those closest to you to believe that which God has whispered in your ear. Abraham agreed to have a child with Sarah's maid Hagar, to appease the anxieties Sarah was facing as she got older. I can imagine Abraham thinking, 'Maybe just maybe that was the way God would fulfil the promise'. Isn't it interesting how things that were difficult to achieve sometimes seem to work out easily when in our fleshy attempts to help God, we step out of the perfect will of God? It's called deception! The enemy offers a temporary fix but if it's not God, it's not good for you! What is not born of God cannot fully manifest the promise of God.

Even Abraham and Sarah's attempt to fix 'the problem' did not undo that which God had spoken. It became a part of the fulfilment of God's word - father of nations. Out of Ishmael, the son of Hagar, would arise a nation and nations would come from the promised son Isaac. What a merciful God we serve!

Abraham and Sarah had a very long wait between God's utterance of the promise and the manifestation of that promise. Not everyone will have 'fast-food' delivery of promises. Fine- dining restaurants produce high-quality food, but the waiting time is usually longer. When divine destiny is connected to your promise the process of waiting is a must. What we sometimes deem to be delay is God processing us to develop the capacity to receive the promise. Waiting forces our flesh and our ego to die. It opens our eyes to the truth of who God is and that he is Sovereign over all. There is revelation, power and transformation in the waiting. Don't waste your waiting period!

The promise was fulfilled. Abraham at 100 years old and Sarah at 90 years old became biological parents with no help from their witty minds, but resting solely on the truth of God. This time the son of promise came forth-Isaac was born; just as God had promised!

Wilderness Treasures:

- **Make a habit of reading the Bible.**

No matter how low you feel or how hopeless your reality appears to be, never stop reading God's word. Never close your heart to His voice through the Scriptures. The word of God is the primary language of the Kingdom of God and the key to access what is in the King's heart for you.

- **Be sensitive to the Holy Spirit.**

Be careful not to miss God because you are led only by your intellect or your emotions and not by the promptings of the Holy Spirit. Be led by the Spirit of God.

- **God's promise is settled.**

Even if you stop believing, God's promise is settled. It is awaiting the development of your faith -the password- to withdraw from the heavenly realms that which is yours, so it can manifest in your life here on earth.

- **Intimacy is grown in a place of vulnerability.**

The wilderness taught me to be open before God. To show Him where it hurt and how badly it hurt, to express my emotions freely, knowing His love could handle it. In those moments, there was an internal, intimate intertwining taking place in my walk with God. My relationship with Him was changing, evolving, strengthening and my faith was growing during my wilderness journey.

My reality was barrenness. God's truth was fruitfulness according to the mandate given to us as humans in Genesis 1 vs. 28 to (among other things) be fruitful and multiply. What a joy to know that our reality, one day, must give way to truth! We must also recognize that our active participation is critical. We must cooperate with God for the fulfillment of his promises in our lives. Passivity does not breed manifestation. Intentionality does.

My reality continued to stare me in the face, so I had to become intentional about constantly beholding the Word of God and feeding my eyes with the truth of God, because we produce and become what we focus on most. Faith comes by hearing and hearing by the word of God (Romans 10 vs. 17). I had to open my heart to the faith boosters God downloaded to me from His word. I encourage you to come into agreement with the truths that God has revealed to you and use them to lay hold on what is rightfully yours. Fight and wait in faith. Do not be intimidated by your reality. Intimidate your reality by declaring and believing Truth!

Luke 21 vs.13

"Faith comes by hearing
and hearing by the
word of God."

Chapter 4

FAITH ACTIVATED

As I write this chapter, I am amazed at just how intentional God is. The Bible declares in Jeremiah 1: 12 that He watches over his word to perform it. The Message version puts it this way *"…I am (actively) watching over My Word to fulfil it."* What does that really mean? From experience, I believe it means that when God speaks a word, He deliberately and purposefully orchestrates things to ensure that word comes to pass. A farmer 'watches over' the seeds he has planted, he waters and nourishes them and sustains an environment for them to burst through their outer core, grow and break through the soil to full manifestation. In Chapter 3, I referred to the use of boosters in agriculture and detailed the scriptural boosters God provided on my journey to motherhood. Activators are also used by farmers. They stimulate multiplication and activation of soil microbes that the plant needs for healthy growth, strength, resistance against hazards in the environment and the production of healthy fruit. Activators stimulate microbes, already in the soil, and activate them to produce nutrients for faster plant growth and productivity.

Using this analogy as I reflect on my journey, the seed of the dream had already been planted in me and faith boosters were constantly there from the Word. It was time for my faith to be activated. It was time to receive activators that would cause my faith to begin to grow, break through the surface and manifest through my thoughts, feelings and actions. Once faith is activated, we think, feel and act differently. Looking back, I can see how God orchestrated divine encounters with persons who were being used by him to push my faith to a higher level. I call them Faith Activators:

Faith Activator 1: Rev. Anthony* - Strategic Praying

Rev. Anthony was my mentor throughout my teenage years and into young adulthood. Because of the prophetic gift he carried, many times he would sense when I was not doing well emotionally or otherwise and was very responsive to any promptings he received from Holy Spirit regarding my welfare. Rev. Anthony knew of the difficulties we were facing regarding bearing a child. One day he called by phone and said he needed to meet with Winston and me urgently. We showed up at his business place the next day, thinking we were going to talk there. He told us, "I need to come to your house today." We boarded his vehicle and headed to our home.

As we sat in the living room, he shared what he sensed God was saying about our situation and read verses from the Bible that would increase our faith to believe that what we desired was no challenge for God. He led us through various prayers of repentance and declarations renouncing generational curses as he was led by the Holy Spirit. He encouraged us to believe God fully. He then prayed a powerful prayer; the anointing was rich in the room, and I could feel that this was a God-ordained moment.

As soon as he finished praying, I heard a sound in my ears that I did not understand and I could not make it stop. I wondered whether I should say something. Before I decided, Rev. Anthony, looked at me and said, "Are you okay?" I told him that I was hearing a baby crying. He smiled and told us that was a good thing;

God had heard our petition. I have never forgotten that experience and in the years that followed I could not forget that sound. God gave me an audible glimpse that day, of the truth that was to be mine. My faith was being activated.

Faith Activator 2: Pastor Wade*- Fruitful Trees

At the time of this encounter, Pastor Wade was not known to me personally. I had seen him minister once and I was in awe at the depth of his delivery of the Word and his passion for God. As one of the Parish Youth Directors for the Church of God of Prophecy, St. Catherine West at that time, I was responsible for travelling with Pastor Wade to provide direction from Spanish Town to the community of Brown's Hall, where we were hosting a One-Day Youth Convention.

It was a Saturday afternoon. The journey to the event was good. We talked occasionally about general topics. I could feel a very strong anointing in his car. The atmosphere felt pregnant with the power of God. Ministry was powerful that day as God poured into the lives of the youth through His servant.

On our way back from the event, Pastor Wade asked me two pointed questions. He said, "Megan, are you married and do you have any children?" My mind begged - 'Oh no do not even go there. I DON'T want to talk about it!' I reluctantly answered his questions, "Yes I have been married for 7 years Sir and no I have no children." He chuckled and said, "Well, I believe I have a prophetic word for you from the Lord." I felt myself bracing for it. He continued, "While ministering at the convention, I got this word, but God told me not to say it in the service because it was not for them. A few minutes ago, He reminded me and led me to ask you those two questions. Megan, the Lord says to tell you that you will have children. You are fruitful, you are not barren; and as a sign to you, the Lord says the very trees on your land will become extremely fruitful as a sign to you that the Lord has spoken and you will be the mother of children."

I felt the presence of God in such a tangible way as he spoke that I didn't know what to do. It was as if God had just taken a seat in the car. Tears filled my eyes. How could I not receive such a word? This pastor knew nothing of my life or my battle, but the Lord had spoken through him to again inject truth and further activate my faith to bring it a little closer to manifestation. I received that word, I believed it and I held on to it.

I can imagine you wondering - did the trees become more fruitful? Yes, they did! At the time I received the prophecy, we were still living at our first home and a few weeks later an orange tree at the back started bearing fruit. The caretaker of the property saw them first and exclaimed that for all the years that tree had been there he had never seen one orange on it. I smiled and thanked God because I remembered the prophetic word. A few months later, we relocated to a home which we eventually bought. I recall the previous owner coming to visit us. She commented that the mango trees normally produced mangoes yearly, but what she was seeing that day was beyond what she was accustomed to. She left with bags of mangoes. The same thing happened to the apple tree and the ackee trees at the back. Everything was bearing in abundance! It was simply amazing and to this day, my fruit trees still bear bountifully - a constant reminder of what God spoke over me that day.

That first encounter was the beginning of a mentorship journey with Pastor Wade. He was sent by God in that season and was also used to fan into flame a greater passion for God's word. As I was mentored, my faith grew, my impact grew and my confidence grew in teaching the word of God and leading praise and worship. Even while going through the wilderness, if you are connected to the persons that God sends into your life, you will grow. Joshua was raised into leadership while serving and learning from Moses in the wilderness. Don't miss your Moses because you are distracted by the discomforts of the wilderness.

Based on the reports from our youth convention earlier that year, Pastor Wade was invited by the Parish Overseer to minister at the Parish Convention. He contacted me asking that I travel with him and his team so he could find the community of Old Harbour Bay easily. I agreed to do so. I was picked up in Spanish Town and this time he had with him a male leader from his church. I was very quiet for the journey, but I noticed that the gentleman beside me was praying softly all the way.

After his session of ministry, Pastor Wade and Bishop Senior were in the pastoral office speaking when Bishop Senior sent for me indicating that they wanted to speak with me. I entered the room wondering what this was about. The gentleman who came with Pastor Wade started speaking as soon as I sat down. God had revealed to him that the enemy was on a mission to destroy my life before the age of 41 and he wanted to do it through childbirth or through the frustration of me not having a child. He asked me if anyone in my family had ever died in childbirth - my grandmother died at age 41 during childbirth. It was on that basis that I had been called into the room because he had shared it with his pastor and the Overseer. The three men stood around me and prayed like their lives depended on it; cancelling a very diabolic plan against my life and my fertility. This had been a divine set up.

Faith Activator 3: Joycelyn Lawson -Fill That Drawer

Joycelyn is a recording artiste and friend who sang at our wedding. One night, she visited the church we attended at the time in Bendon, Jamaica to perform at a gospel concert. She had her firstborn daughter with her, who was just a few months old. As she performed, I held the baby. It felt heavenly and I treasured every minute of it. I knew persons were watching me and probably making comments but I really didn't care much.

Joycelyn left shortly after her performance and I realised that she had forgotten the baby's towel on my lap. I quickly got my cell phone and called her to let her know. She chuckled a bit and said, "Meggy take that towel, clear out a drawer at home and place it in there. It's the first gift for you to place in your baby's drawer. Fill it as you prepare for your blessing". I laughed, thanked her and ended the call wondering if I had the faith to actually do that. For days I had the towel sitting there in my guest room until finally one day I emptied a drawer and placed it inside. At that time, I knew nothing about prophetic actions but I now know that that's exactly what it was! A prophetic action is something done to activate a word that God has released over your life.

After a while, I started purchasing small items each month and placing them in the drawer- baby bottles, clothes, toys etc. and I dated each one. I remember vividly one afternoon after leaving work I went into a store and ordered a set of nipple bottles. As the attendant gave me my goods she shouted in true Jamaican style- "You pregnant?!" Okaaay…hmmm. "No." I replied, as embarrassed as could be and exited the store, my bag in hand. I continued the habit and in future months and years, when my faith went low, I would open that drawer and look at all the things I had bought - faith was activated as God watched over His word to perform it.

If you are really believing God for a blessing do prophetic actions towards that blessing. Give your faith hands and feet! James 4:26 states, *"Faith by itself, if it does not have works is dead."*

Faith Activator 4: Tanesha Johnson - Books to Read

Tanesha is a lifelong friend who attended the same church as I did and because of the relationship we had, she knew of the days when I felt alone and forgotten in the wilderness; the days that were spent crying and fighting to hold on to faith. Tanesha always, always told me to have faith. "You are going to be a mother." she would often say. I remember her saying she understood that my faith was running low but on those days, she would continue to have faith on my behalf. What faith!

One Sunday, Tanesha brought me a package at church, it contained two books: 'What to Expect When You're Expecting and What to Expect During the First Year." She said she was led to buy them for me to use when I got pregnant! I love reading and as I read I felt greater hope. I felt like I was being prepared for something big. It no longer felt like oppression; it felt like preparation. Another faith activator had moved in obedience to God. My faith was growing in a season when the enemy expected it to fail. To God be all the glory!

Faith Activator #5: Pastor Greenland*-Generational Cycle Broken

It was a hot and windy Jamaica afternoon; I had just left the bank and was heading home to rest after a tiring day at work. I was out of it though, numb to everything and everyone around me because again I was dealing with the disappointment of not being pregnant. While in the line at the bank I whispered a prayer, "God send me help or I will die from a broken heart".

The taxis that would take me home were parked along a stretch of small business places. I went to a clear spot just in front of a spice and seasoning shop and began waiting patiently for the 'right' car to take me home. I wandered off again into the sea of negative thoughts that were plaguing me…

"Good afternoon." Came a sharp interruption to my mental rambling. I turned quickly as the two words jolted me back to reality. It was a dark gentleman who seemed firm but kind. I responded to his greeting and turned to continue my thinking. He started asking questions like how was your day and do you know that Jesus loves you? My response was a sarcastic question, "Does He?"

To that he responded, "Come inside let's talk." I didn't know this man, but I couldn't not respond. I felt myself following him inside the store but couldn't explain why. It felt like I was compelled to go into this business place with a man I had never met before! It was a small store but Pastor Greenland found an area where we could sit and talk as his workers moved about busily attending to customers.

The amazing thing is he told me that a few minutes earlier, he was sitting in his office and the Holy Spirit told him to get up and go stand at the entrance of his business place because there was a young lady there that he needed to reach.

That conversation was the beginning of a season of learning, insight and freedom. Rev Greenland was a committed servant of God who was anointed to identify generational patterns and cycles that need to be broken. Little did I know that there was a generational cycle operating against the blessing I was to walk into. As we talked and he probed my background and family history my eyes were opened to several things. I will share one main one for the benefit of those of you who may be fighting a battle you are unaware of.

I am told that as a baby I was very 'delicate'. A paternal grand-aunt with the best of intentions told my mother that she should name me after my deceased paternal grandmother…my pet name therefore became Evie and to be honest I quite liked it.

My grandmother though she had five children had a constant battle with childbearing -resulting in the death of her sixth child as an infant and her own death and the death of the seventh child during childbirth. My aunt, her first daughter, had a similar battle but luckily had not lost her life. She has two children but had suffered at least 3 traumatic miscarriages.

I was the first daughter for my parents and the battle arose again in the same area - fertility and childbirth…but God! As the pattern became clearer and clearer, my faith in God's ability to end the cycle grew. Now I know that God reveals to heal. The next step was for us to be strategic and intentional with the information God had revealed to us Rev Greenland instructed us to go into a period of prayer and fasting and guided us as to how to pray regarding this. We then met with him and his wife one afternoon for prayer and deliverance.

Some Christians are opposed to deliverance because of their understanding and perception of it. My current pastor and spiritual father, Apostle Dr. Courtney McLean in his book, Demonology Volume 1, states, *"Deliverance refers to salvation, liberation, release, rescue, emancipation and redemption. Jesus emphasizes deliverance of the captives as an integral part of His ministry. Deliverance for the captives is synonymous with the granting of freedom for those bound by satanic oppression. It speaks to the undoing of the works of the devil within the lives of individuals." (Mclean, 2019. P. 31)* The believer cannot be possessed by the enemy because the Spirit of God lives in him/her; however, the believer can be oppressed where the enemy seeks to manipulate or control certain areas of the believer's life.

Thank God for the authority we have through the blood and the name of Jesus Christ to break chains, disrupt ungodly cycles and demolish evil strongholds! Hallelujah!

I left the session with Pastor Greenland and his wife that day with a knowing in my heart that the generational cycle no longer had power over me. It was broken.

Faith Activators #6: The Morrisons - Gifts for the Baby

I always enjoy sharing this part of my journey. The Morrisons were a couple from our church. Our friendship had grown over the years and they had two children and told us several times they would be having no more. Their children were like ours. My husband and I were home one afternoon we heard a vehicle at the gate and realized it was theirs. As Winston and I headed towards them, Mr Morrison stepped out of the vehicle and opened the car trunk. His wife exited as well and started smiling. To my surprise, they started taking things from the car. "These are yours. Put them in the baby's room." Mrs. Morrison said smiling.

For a few seconds I didn't know how to respond but I knew her well enough to know that she wasn't joking. They had brought us a baby's car seat, a play pen and a baby stroller- a complete set. I didn't know how to process this. It was one of the most potent moves God had made so far in the scheme of things and one of the greatest confrontations between what God had declared versus what the doctors had spoken. While I couldn't fully explain it, I knew I had to accept those gifts as I knew they were being led by God and this was not an ordinary move. They confirmed that they had prayed about it and they sensed God saying they should take the items to us and so they obeyed. We talked a bit and before she left Mrs Morrison hugged me and reminded me that God would do it.

That night it took a while for me to sleep. I kept getting up to look at the gifts we had just received. Was this a dream? My Heavenly Father would not set me up like this to leave me childless…something was brewing… I could feel it and I was now seeing it. I felt a knowing in my heart - faith being activated.

Wilderness Treasures:

- **Connections Matter.**

Even while going through the wilderness, if you are connected to the ones God sends into your life, you will grow.

- **Faith Activators appear in wilderness seasons too.**

Don't miss your destiny helpers, your deliverers, your Moses because you are distracted by the discomforts of the wilderness. Always remember that God can send help at any time and through anyone. They are sent to activate your faith and help position you for the manifestation of the promise.

- **God reveals to deal.**

When God uncovers a strategy of the enemy, it is a sign that he is ready to address it and shift your life. Cooperate with Him!

- **God watches over His words in your life.**

God is not a man that He should lie. It is His intention to deliver that which He has promised you and He actively watches over it in various ways.

Writing this chapter has been such a blessing! We have a Heavenly Father who actively walks with us through every wilderness experience. If we allow Him, He leads us through the wilderness and as we yield to the process we don't just go through it, we grow through it. And what the enemy meant for evil God turns it around for our good. God was strategic in all he was doing. I was being prepared for the years ahead.

May you trust God in the waiting place and may every Faith Activator that you need show up in your life on time and on divine assignment!

Chapter 5

FAITH TESTED

THE CRUCIBLE OF DISAPPOINTMENT

It was November 2007 and I wasn't feeling well physically. I was queasy, bloated and very lethargic. Could it be that I was pregnant after so many years of waiting? I decided to wait for a few more days before I checked.

After several days of strange symptoms I decided to do a pregnancy test one day while Winston was at work. That way if it was another false alarm I could keep it to myself. I was two months into my full-time study pursuing my master's degree in counselling psychology, so I was home alone most days. Five minutes seemed like forever as I waited to check the results on the pregnancy test and to my surprise it was positive! I sat in my couch holding the test in my hand for several minutes. This was really happening! I wanted to call Winston immediately. I needed to tell someone but somehow, I decided to wait and to let it sink in. After dinner, when he was relaxed, I gave him the kit in a tiny box. Words fail me now to describe the look on his face when he saw what was inside - we hugged, we prayed, we worshipped. It felt surreal.

For the next few weeks, we were engaged in seeing a gynaecologist in the town nearest to where we lived and getting preliminary checks done. We decided not to say anything to anyone. It would be our secret - at least for now. All seemed to be going well based on the blood tests and ultrasound. The Christmas season was now upon us and I had some uncomfortable symptoms including intermittent cramps. All efforts to reach the doctor I had seen initially were futile. Each time I called her office I was told that she was busy and that she did not give out her personal number. I went there one day but was told I could not see her without an appointment so I should come back on my next appointment date. In a discussion with a good friend Dahlia, I told her I was pregnant but that I had a gut feeling I needed to get a check-up before my next scheduled doctor's visit which was four weeks away. She suggested that I follow that gut feeling and gave me a number to call her gynaecologist's office. I did that the next day and after one visit with Dr. Sharmaine Mitchell I decided to forget the first gynaecologist I had visited. Dr. Mitchell was warm, welcoming and seemed to understand my anxiety based on my 9 years of waiting. As we were about to leave the office, she handed me a paper with her number and said, "Call me anytime."

I was asked to minister the Word at my church on Youth Sunday - the last Sunday in January 2009. As I sought the Lord regarding a topic, I heard "A Change is Coming". For days I kept listening to the song by Kevin Downswell of the same title as I prepared to share the word:

"A change is coming. Can you feel the burning? Yes, I know that the season is turning; it's turning! A Change is Coming!"

On the morning of the sermon, I still felt unwell in my body but I was determined to share the word I believe God had laid on my heart for his people, particularly because my change had come and I wanted to encourage someone else. I was almost twelve weeks pregnant but it was not yet obvious to anyone.   As I shared the Word I wondered if the congregants were receiving it. On what basis was I qualified to encourage them about expecting a change? I was the lady waiting to get pregnant for almost nine years! I squared my shoulders and delivered the word I received from the Lord. Who was I to question Him? I was His servant- my duty was to obey.

At our second visit to Dr. Mitchell, we were instructed to do an ultrasound and return with the results. By then I was about 14 weeks pregnant and everything seemed perfect. We were excited to see this little gift on screen. It all felt like a dream. Tears filled my eyes as I saw the little person growing inside me. It was too early to know the gender but I was looking at my miracle!

I soon noticed that the radiologist had a look of concern on her face. "Is everything okay?" I asked. No answer. "Is everything okay?" She looked at me and reassured me that all was well but insisted that I should head back to Dr. Mitchell with the results immediately. I felt like a huge lump was in my throat when she said that. I wished I could run away from what I felt was unfolding.

The drive back to Dr. Mitchell was long and silent. In her office, I could feel my heart beating in my chest as she read the report silently. Then she began to explain what was happening as calmly as she could. She told us that it seemed I was heading into early labour as the cervix was opening but she could try to prevent that with an emergency cerclage procedure. 'Wait…WHAT???!!!' I thought. I was freaking out inside but I tried to maintain my composure. I didn't even know what a cerclage was! Dr. Mitchell explained that it was a stitch placed around the cervix to keep it closed and give my baby a fighting chance. We would need to pay and be registered at the hospital for surgery that same night.

In that moment I would have given anything to wake up and find out that it was all a bad dream. The doctor gave us instructions and information including the cost of this emergency procedure. We quickly headed to a nearby ATM machine to check how much money we had available. To our dismay, it was not enough to cover the costs. What were we supposed to do now? This was just crazy! I called Dr. Mitchell and told her the situation. She said the surgery had to go on, so we should pay the hospital fees and hers could be paid later. Our next step was to go to the University Hospital of the West Indies, doctor's referral in hand. The next few hours seemed like an eternity as I felt like I was racing against time. I went through numerous tests, regular blood pressure checks, and another ultrasound which required no food.

At approximately 10:55 p.m. I was prepared for the operation theatre and as I was wheeled away on the stretcher I could feel my heart racing wildly again. This was happening way too fast. My husband, Winston hugged me and reassured me that he was praying. The next voice I heard was Dr. Mitchell's: "I am here Megan… relax it's going to be fine…"

I woke up a few hours later in some pain, but the nurses told me that the procedure went well. I was sent home the next day, with strict instructions including two week's bed rest. For the next seven months I was to avoid heavy housework, lifting and sex! Okaaay then… Grace Lord! At this point, we were both determined to make whatever sacrifice necessary to save our baby.

During the next few days, we told a few close relatives and friends especially those we knew would agree with us in prayer. Our doctor's visit two weeks after the procedure indicated that all was well; things seemed to be coming together nicely and the candle of our hope kept flickering.

"AAAAHHHH!" My scream pelted the silence of the midnight hour and Winston woke up alarmed. A few seconds earlier I woke up in excruciating pain and felt the need to use the bathroom. While returning I felt a heavy gush of fluid flow from my body and I knew I was in trouble. Winston found me standing in the passage tears rolling down my cheeks as I cried loudly, staring at him in fear. He realised what was happening, ran for my phone and called Dr Mitchell's number. She told us to head straight to the hospital as this was an emergency. It was almost 1 a.m. the roads were empty and my husband sped like a rocket to Kingston that morning. Every second felt like an hour though as the pain grew more intense.

"Why is this happening to me? No this must be a dream. God, you have to help me!" were some thoughts flying through my head. When we got to the emergency room , preliminary checks were being done but Dr. Mitchell called and instructed them to have me admitted. Early the next morning Dr Mitchell called and told me what to expect that day. I would be taken off the ward to do an ultrasound to determine if any amniotic fluid was left and to determine the status of the baby. I dreaded all of that but there was no escape.

As the ultrasound was being done, I hoped for good news. I remembered the first time I had seen my baby just about 2 weeks ago and the joy I had felt. I was jolted back to my present reality when I heard the radiologist and the nurse discussing what they were seeing No water was left in the sac. The baby was intact, but the heartbeat was extremely low. It seemed it was just a matter of time before that little heartbeat would go silent forever.

I felt my heart sink. I could feel my emotions plunging into a deep dark hole…everything else was a blur for the rest of the day. This was just too much for me to handle. I know now, I really wasn't handling it, I could not have handled it - my Shepherd was carrying me through it.

Later that day, Dr. Mitchell came to visit me and in her usual reassuring tone, she encouraged me to believe. She told me of miraculous cases when the body reproduced brand new fluid and babies were not lost. As any good doctor would, she also encouraged me that if things didn't go well there was hope to do this again. I tried to digest all that I was hearing but it was extremely difficult. The next 24 hours in the hospital were marked with regular checks on the baby's heartbeat and my blood pressure which by now had started to elevate.

By the following morning the verdict was in, there was no heartbeat. Our little one had died. My stomach hurt from a deep inner place and I felt myself curl under the sheets and tears began to flow. I cried from the very deepest core of my being, I cried but the pain only intensified. The emotional pain I felt was beyond words and nothing it seems could stop it. The nurses tried to comfort me but realised there was nothing they could do. They drew the curtains and allowed me to cry for as long as I needed to. Facing the reality of a miscarriage is one of the most painful experiences a mother or father can ever go through; and many misunderstand it.

Word spread quickly both in our families and within the church circle that Megan had lost a baby. Phone calls started coming in but

I was not ready to talk. My baby was still in my womb and the doctors informed that I would have to go through labour and delivery to get him out. First, they waited for my body to naturally go into labour but nothing happened. I was given oral tablets, IV's, inserts but still another 48 hours and no labour. Dr. Mitchell was becoming concerned as she said my womb was now in danger for infection and permanent damage.

In spite of my grief, I realised at that point that this was warfare. Not only was the enemy after this baby but also my ability to become a mother. He was after my womb! I grabbed my phone and began texting specific persons including my then pastor, Rev Cecelia Bailey (now deceased) and some of the Faith Activators I mentioned earlier: Rev. Anthony, Pastor Wade, Pastor Greenland. Prayers started going up, intense prayers, consistent prayers. Some persons were so deliberate they came to the hospital and prayed. Others called and prayed on the phone. Some battles require reinforcement - too much was at stake.

I recall one lady, Ms. Walters, who worked at the hospital. She was asked by Pastor Wade to come and pray with me. The optimism that flowed from her was almost daunting. She encouraged me to trust God. She was convinced that I would get through this and that my womb was blessed. She prayed for me commanding labour to start as my womb must not be damaged and then left to return to her work post. About 15 minutes after she prayed, I started having intermittent intense pain and the nurses confirmed that I was finally going into labour. Yes, it is true, the prayers of righteous men and women are powerful and effective! (James 5 vs. 16).

If you are a woman reading this and you have had a similar experience then you know how difficult it is to have to give birth to a baby that will not move, cry, squeeze your finger or look you in the eyes. The more I pushed the more emotional pain I felt. Why was I going through this, for nothing? I felt like God had taken a long walk somewhere and I was left to do this alone. I know that wasn't true but that's what it felt like. There are some experiences in life that even if they want to, no human can truly walk through it with you. My husband stood by me holding my hand, but I was the one lying on that bed screaming in pain knowing there was no joy at the end of this labour process. At one point it got too much for Winston and he walked out of the section I was in and sat on a chair nearby, checking on me every now and again.

Listen, never ever believe that fathers don't hurt too when they lose a baby. They do! I understood and I was okay with him stepping away. The nurse assigned to me kept coming and going too. In retrospect I believe she too saw that my cries were as much due to emotional pain as they were physical. I was emotionally and physically drained after almost 2 hours. My body was not cooperating and I had to use my will power to push that baby out. I felt like I was now fighting for my womb. I was racing against time because the doctors suspected an infection was brewing as my white blood cells had increased significantly.

Finally, I felt the tiny baby crown and almost four hours after labour had started, he was finally born at 6:55 pm on February 26, 2008. Yes, it was a boy. A very tiny but precious baby boy. I could see his little arms and legs, his head and his face-to me he was beautiful. The nurse asked if I wanted to hold him and I said yes. For almost 10 minutes I sat there holding him, looking at him, touching his fingers and wishing I could have kept him safe-tears running down my cheeks. It was heart-wrenching- a moment in time that felt like the whole world had stopped as I was faced with a reality I had dreaded for so long. The baby I had believed for was gone and I could do nothing to bring him back. I named him

Samuel Andrew and reluctantly released him and allowed the nurse to take him away.

THE AFTERMATH

The ringing of my phone woke me up and as soon as I opened my eyes I recalled what I had gone through a few hours earlier. It seemed I had been given medication to make me sleep. Winston was sitting on the chair next to my bed looking at me almost expressionless. I answered the phone and heard Dr Mitchell's voice. She empathised, checked on how I was doing and updated me on what would happen the next morning. I would have to do a final procedure called a D & C to ensure that all fragments of the pregnancy were removed from my body. I still felt like I was in a bad dream and wanted someone, anyone, to wake me up. I thanked Dr. Mitchell and ended the call.

The next morning, I was taken to the labour and delivery ward for the D & C, procedure which was very uncomfortable and further intensified my emotional pain. I wanted it to end quickly so that I could leave the labour ward because I was hearing women in labour, newborn babies crying, mothers reacting to holding their baby for the first time and I was empty-handed and broken-hearted.

As I was being prepared to be taken back to my ward, a nurse came and stood behind the wheelchair I was in. I thought to myself, 'Yes. I can finally get out of this place - it's too much!' "Mrs, Hylton," she said, interrupting my thoughts of relief, "Dr. Mitchell just called and asked me to give you a tour of the ward before I take you back downstairs." "No, no, it's okay," I responded. "That's fine." "I have to," she insisted. "Dr. Mitchell said I should show you around and let you know you will be back here very soon." "Me…yea right." I mumbled.

My short but very detailed tour of the labour ward began and the nurse was deliberate in her discourse. I was shown the examination room, the labour ward, the delivery rooms and the doors that led to the operating theatre. I still recall some of her words: "This is the examination room where you will be checked when you first come here, then as labour progresses you will be on the labour ward. When you are ready to deliver the baby, we will move you to one of the delivery rooms and those big doors lead to the operating theatre. We only take you there if you have to do a C-section."

When she was satisfied that I had seen enough she took me back to my bed on Ward 11 reminding me that I would soon be back to have my baby there. In the moment, I could not understand why Dr. Mitchell would want me to get a tour of the labour ward, but I had grown to trust her. I didn't think I needed that at the time but in retrospect I realise that God was again watering my faith. In the coming months the memory of that labour ward would not leave my mind and the words 'you will be back soon' kept echoing somewhere deep in my soul. I was discharged the next day.

The days that followed my leaving the hospital were extremely challenging to say the least. It was difficult for both Winston and me to accept that we were no longer pregnant - that the baby we had felt moving just a few days earlier was now a memory. We dealt with the loss differently. Winston didn't get time off from work so most days I was home alone. I literally felt like a zombie - everything was hazy, like a bad dream I could not get out of. He was also grieving but his focus was ensuring that I was okay. He distracted himself with work. We talked less to each other, but we tried our best not to stop communicating totally. I soon realised that he preferred not to talk about the details of what had happened, so I tried to talk about other things. To get through that period, we needed to understand and support each other and thankfully, God granted us the wisdom to do so.

We had several visits from family members, friends, church leaders and brethren, many of whom understood that there was not much they could say to ease our pain but that their presence was what we needed most. There were others who sent messages of encouragement and hope by phone, which were very helpful. Unfortunately, there were those persons who had their own theories and explanations for why we had lost the baby. Some even alluded to God telling them the reason. I honestly prefer if they had kept those explanations to themselves as they did more harm to me than good.

During the days, I managed fairly well due to visitors, messages, and phone calls; but the nights were really hard as I found myself alone with my thoughts and sleep continued to evade me for weeks. I would lie in bed wondering why this had to be a part of our story. I would get up and write in my journal sometimes or I would create a song on spot to get my emotions out and record it on my phone. Other nights I wondered how Winston could manage to sleep at a time like this and I couldn't? (The guy was tired Megan!). Overall, it was a period of emotional and mental turmoil. I went into therapy for a few weeks to help me work through the myriad of thoughts and emotions I was experiencing. It was a traumatic experience that I didn't want to get stuck in. Eventually, I resolved in my heart that I would put my best foot and face forward when I needed to and battle the hurt and the disappointment at home when I was alone.

I was in my second year of Graduate school, and having been traumatised by the loss of the baby, I was in a battle for my mind and my joy. My greatest weapons were journaling and listening to worship songs. Those songs had a calming effect on me and from that place of calm I would express my feelings in my journal. Journalling is a proven effective tool for some persons to express their deepest thoughts and feelings about an issue especially one of a personal nature. I found an outlet in my journal and I used it regularly. I used it to express to God what I could not bring myself to say out loud. I had not prayed since the day my son died in my womb. That day I had said to God, "I don't know what to say to You right now Father and I don't want to sin against You, so I have nothing to say."

My daily routine was to do whatever came to mind. I was on sick leave for about two weeks but I was granted some extra time to heal. Depression had blanketed me again like a thick dark cloud and everywhere I went I felt covered by it. I knew that depression was among the five stages of grief but what I was feeling was so heavy it was almost making it literally difficult to breathe.

One morning, while at home, Pastor Wade called to check on me. We spoke a bit and then he asked if I had talked to God yet. I told him no. He replied, "Megan, God can handle your pain; He says to tell you He can handle your pain." He allowed a few seconds for that to sink in then instructed me to close the windows and doors of my house and tell God exactly how I was feeling. That prayer, he said, would mark the beginning of my healing process.

"Go. He's waiting on you…" he said softly before ending the call. I sat for a while and wondered if it was worth the try. The pain I had inside was beginning to feel unbearable. I walked through my house and closed every door and every window. I got down on the floor before God. I was there for almost two hours-tears, words, groanings, tears, words, groanings. I held nothing back, I told him everything-the anger, the disappointment, the fears, the hurt, the guilt, the shame… and for what it was still worth, the hope. There began the healing process towards the restoration of my faith.

Six weeks after the miscarriage I had an appointment with Dr. Mitchell at her office at the University Hospital of the West Indies (UHWI). When I arrived, there were several pregnant women in the waiting room and others who had their newborn babies. As I sat in the room I began to feel overwhelmed by what I was seeing and hearing. Questions flooded my mind-why couldn't I have my baby like they did? Why did it have to end that way? Didn't I deserve to be blessed with a child? It got so bad that I decided to get up and wait in the passage where I would see less persons.

A few minutes later Dr. Mitchell arrived and as she walked by me, she indicated that I should follow her. I was one of the first patients she saw that day because she knew it was no easy task being there at that time. Again, she used the opportunity to encourage me to keep on believing God to turn things around. She emphasized, "Now we know what the challenges are and how to plan for those challenges for your next baby. You will be fine."

I honestly believe that God chose Dr. Mitchell for me. She understood my pain but she never entertained doubt and unbelief. I needed that kind of a doctor. Associations matter when growing through the wilderness. You need to have the right people speaking into your ear as what you absorb can serve to abort your destiny or give life to it. I was learning to believe God in every circumstance. My pain was real, my heart was broken, healing would take God and time.

Wilderness Treasures:

- **Mixed emotions.**

In a season of grief, you will experience mixed emotions. You have not lost your faith; you are human and having lost someone of value you will grieve.

- **Sift through advice.**

Some persons will say the wrong things with the right intentions. Sift through what is good for you and ignore what makes no sense.

- **God can handle your pain.**

Our Heavenly Father invites you to cast all your cares on Him, because He cares for you.

- **Healing after trauma takes time.**

Be intentional about your healing but give yourself grace as you heal.

This, I believe was the most difficult chapter to write. Does that mean I am not yet healed? No. It means I am human and as a human some memories can be difficult to revisit. As I reflected and read through my journals, I recall one truth that I discovered as God was healing my heart. As painful as it was at the time to lose him, little Samuel fulfilled his purpose. He came just for a short time but he helped us discover the avenue the enemy was trying to use to prevent me from having children. The approach going forward would be different, but the focus was first healing and wholeness.

Chapter 6

COPING AFTER A MISCARRIAGE

UNDERSTANDING MISCARRIAGE

Having gone through two miscarriages, I learned firsthand how emotionally crippling they can be. Miscarriages are very common. Research suggests that 1 in every 8 pregnancies end in a miscarriage. The harsh reality is that many women and men have had to carry their pain silently. Left unaddressed, this kind of bereavement has the potential to eat away at the soul like a fast-spreading cancer eventually sucking the joy out of life.

A miscarriage is one of the most silent losses a woman can experience. It often comes without warning, without clear explanations, and without the communal rituals that normally accompany grief. Many women quietly carry the weight of unanswered questions, wondering *why* it happened and whether their bodies failed them in some way.

Medically, the word miscarriage refers to the loss of a pregnancy, during the first trimester or at least before 23 weeks. The possible causes are varied and, in many cases, unknown. Some losses occur due to chromosomal abnormalities in the baby's development causing the body to automatically shed the pregnancy. Other causes may include hormonal imbalances, underlying health conditions, infections, uterine or cervical issues, or extreme physical stress. In some instances, despite thorough medical evaluation, no definitive cause is ever identified. This uncertainty can deepen the grief, leaving women searching for meaning where there may be no clearcut answers.

A miscarriage usually impacts the body, the mind, and the spirit. Physically, a woman may experience bleeding, cramping, fatigue, hormonal shifts, breast tenderness, and changes in appetite or sleep. These symptoms may last for days or weeks, and they can be emotionally triggering - each physical symptom echoing the loss. Hormonal changes can also intensify mood swings, tearfulness, anxiety, and a sense of emotional fragility.

Psychologically and emotionally, the effects often linger far longer. Many women report feelings of shock, denial, sadness, guilt, anger, emptiness, and deep disappointment. There may be grief not only for the baby, but for the future that was imagined, the names chosen, the milestones anticipated, the identity of becoming a mother again or for the first time. Some women experience intrusive thoughts, heightened anxiety about future pregnancies, or a sense of isolation when others minimize the loss or expect them to "move on" quickly.

Spiritually, a miscarriage can shake one's faith. Questions may arise that feel uncomfortable to voice: *Where was God? Why would He allow this? Did I miss something? Am I being punished for something I did in the past?* These questions are not signs of weak faith; they are expressions of a wounded heart searching for understanding. Scripture reminds us that God is close to the broken-hearted, even when His ways cannot be understood.

A miscarriage has a way of silencing a room and a heart. There are no adequate words, no rehearsed responses for the moment when you realize the baby you were carrying will not be going home with you. I remember the stillness - the kind that feels loud. I remember the confusion, the numbness, the pain and feeling that no one, absolutely no one understood exactly what I was going through. And maybe I was right, because each person's experience of losing an unborn child is unique.

THE GRIEF NO ONE SEES

Being the mother who lost the baby is different from knowing the mother who lost the baby. What surprised me most was how invisible the grief of a miscarriage felt. 'You never had a baby in the first place so why is it such a big deal?' is how those who have never walked the path may view it. And so, I learned quickly that a woman often grieves her loss quietly, privately and sometimes alone because the people around her downplay the intensity of the loss. As you will see in the next chapter, some persons expected me to 'get over this' and get back to normal functioning quickly but it really is not that simple.

Life around me continued as normal but my life could not continue as normal. I was mourning more than a pregnancy. I didn't lose a pregnancy; I lost a son. I was mourning timelines, expectations, a due date that would never come and a version of myself that believed that my turning point had arrived. I was mourning prayers I thought were finally answered and prophetic words I thought were being fulfilled.

Just two weeks after the loss, my supervisor at the church office, who was also a trained counsellor and pastor, invited Winston and me to spend a weekend at her home in the country. She knew my love for nature and felt that getting away for a few days would provide some solace for us. She was right. The weekend was heavenly. Greenery was all around. We had our own flat upstairs which had a jacuzzi. She didn't allow us to cook, our meals were prepared and taken to us. All we had to do was relax and rest. It was a welcomed break and we were extremely grateful.

During that weekend I found a book to read that I could not put down for long. It was entitled, *Breaking Ungodly Soul Ties*. I read the entire book and left with a resolve in my heart: I was not going create an ungodly tie with the trauma I had gone through. It was still early days but in my heart I decided I would not get stuck here. The stillness of that weekend also stilled my heart before God and I could feel Him offering me His love and comfort.

WRESTLING WITH GOD AND STAYING

As a woman of faith, I never imagined that I would have faced such a significant loss on my journey to motherhood. I had prayed, hoped, and believed long before this child was conceived. So, when life finally began to grow within me, it felt like heaven had responded and my story was about to change for the better. Then, with no warning whatsoever, everything changed. In one moment, I was basking in the joy of the tender movements within me; the next moment I was fighting frantically to save his life.

I struggled with questions I didn't know how to say out loud. *Lord, why would You allow me to conceive only to lose it? Did I hear You wrong? Was my faith not enough? Were the prophetic words true? Would my story ever change? Was it my fault?*

Even after the encounter where I poured my heart out to God and healing started, there were moments when prayer felt heavy and scripture felt distant. But thank God for grace. Even when I wanted to get up and walk away from God - I stayed. I didn't stay because

I was strong; I stayed because His strength is made perfect when I am weakest. He caused me to stay. May God cause you to stay with Him, even when you don't understand; even when your questions are unanswered. Stay. There is no safer place or person to lean on in your lowest moments than God. I eventually learned that faith does not mean the absence of questions. It means bringing them honestly before God knowing He is sovereign and He knows all things and He is my Father.

God never dismissed my questions or rebuked my tears. He met me in them, comforted me through them and healed me from them. As painful as the process was, those times of praying, crying and questioning were birthing another level of intimacy between my heavenly father and me. He ultimately became my hiding place. When the people around me did not understand, I could run to him. He was proving to be a very present help in my time of trouble.

RELEASING THE BURDEN OF SELF-BLAME

One of the greatest mental battles a woman faces after a miscarriage is the burden of self-blame. In the quiet moments when questions flood the mind, guilt tries to take root. Conversations, decisions, activities are re-played as she wonders if she missed something or did something wrong. This is especially difficult if there is no obvious medical explanation for the loss.

Eventually I had to release responsibility for something I could not control and stop blaming myself for something that really was not my fault. I got to this point over time, by reading and gaining knowledge on the challenges I had during the pregnancy.

HOLDING ON TO MY IDENTITY

After the miscarriage, I wondered what God was forming in me during the waiting. Romans 8 vs. 28 is a verse I take literally: *"And we know that all things work together for good to them that love God; to them who are called according to His purpose."* I knew that God was forming something out of this and though I had no answers yet-it was working for my good. I realized that although I experienced great loss, my purpose was not lost. My purpose was bigger than my pain. This part of the journey taught me over time that God's promises are not erased by pain or tragedy. Sometimes they are refined by pain and tragedy. I was still called, still chosen, still anointed, still loved, still held, still valued.

FINDING AN OUTLET

Coping after a miscarriage can be like a roller coaster ride with no fixed duration. Some days you may feel like you are doing better and then suddenly you wake up and you are flat on your face again emotionally or you encounter a trigger and it evokes emotions you thought you had learned to manage. I had to learn to navigate these mountain and valley days and extend grace to myself. Accepting that I had gone through a traumatic experience and being human meant I would have some up days and some down days and I had to be okay with that. The emotions and thoughts needed a voice, they needed to be expressed and thankfully I discovered ways to do that.

Finding the right outlets often determines how soon some women bounce back after a miscarriage. And don't get me wrong, bouncing back does not mean forgetting what happened or pretending that nothing happened. Bouncing back means accepting what has happened but being willing and able to live again, dream again, be again.

My first outlet was trusted friends and mentors. I have always had a small inner circle and they were the ones who provided an ear for me to voice how I felt with no fear of judgment. Secondly, I reached out for help. I told the director of my programme of study what had happened and she arranged for me to receive therapy. I spent two months in therapy and it was very helpful in helping me process my pain and explore how to navigate the days ahead.

Journalling was my third outlet and I must say as I have had to read through my journals as I write this book, I realize just how much I went through and how much I offloaded on to those pages. I wrote about how I felt, what I was thinking, my experiences and what I sensed God was saying to me. My fourth outlet and undoubtedly the most effective was prayer. In the aftermath of losing Samuel, prayer evolved into an ongoing conversation with God. I Thessalonians 5 vs. 17 says, "Pray without ceasing." Prayer was no longer a duty I had to perform it was a knowing that God is always with me in every single moment, despite what I was facing He was there and I could talk with him and he spoke to me, Hallelujah!

Journal entry: March 24, 2008

"Tribute to Samuel Andrew."

When I think about you, it pains my heart
To know that so soon we had to part.
We never got the chance to share a smile
To hold a hand or snuggle for a while.
I used to dream of holding you near,
Of telling you how precious you were my dear.

My dreams for you will never come true,
I had to let you go and say adieu.
It's really not clear when my pain will end,
When the tears will stop flowing
And my heart will mend.
But I know I do love you
Just as much as when you were here
And I am sure the Saviour has you
In His tender loving care.

You really didn't belong to me
Your presence was to prove
That God had heard my prayers'

And He will surely bring me through

Your time here was very short

You never saw a sunrise

Or felt the touch of pain

You never cringed, you never cried

All you knew was peace.

I'll always wonder what you would have been like

Your eyes, your ears, your nose,

Your laugh, your touch, your personality, your talents and your pose.

My dear Sumuel I am sorry

We'll never live our dream

But please be sure I love you so…I really really do.

I don't think I will ever forget you

I can't get you out of my mind

But I believe you'd want me to try again

And have more peace of mind.

So go on my child – live and be free

Within heaven's gates of eternity

God wants you to be free

So be the best that you can be –

bring glory to His name

I cheer you on my little one

You've entered the hall of fame.

I'll see you when my purpose is done
I must finish my race too
Until then I must be strong
There's more for me to do.
It's hard to move another step
But the Saviour holds my hand
I will not die; I will live and declare
His ever perfect plan.
My womb is blessed and so I know
It shall bring forth joy and laughter
And sons and daughters shall be born to me
In this precious life.
Live and be free my dear child
Your journey's just begun
Live on, like the wind
Be free, be free, for all eternity.

M. Hylton

HEALING AFTER A MISCARRIAGE

One of the most common questions women ask after a miscarriage is, *How long will it take to heal?* The honest answer is that healing is not linear, nor does it follow a fixed timeline. Each woman heals in her own time and at her own pace and this can depend on how attached she was to the baby lost, how much she had wanted the pregnancy and how she perceives the miscarriage overall. Physical recovery may take several weeks, depending on the stage of pregnancy and the woman's overall health. Emotional and spiritual healing, however, usually unfolds in layers, gradually.

Some women feel a sense of emotional steadiness within months; others find that waves of grief return unexpectedly on due dates, anniversaries, at baby showers, or when seeing other children reach milestones their baby never did. Healing does not mean forgetting. It means learning how to carry the loss without it defining or disabling you.

Support plays a critical role in this process. Healing is not meant to happen in isolation. Trusted support may include a compassionate spouse or partner, a close friend who listens without fixing, a counsellor or therapist trained in grief or reproductive loss, a faith leader who offers spiritual covering, or a support group of women who understand this unique pain. There is something deeply restorative about being seen and heard without judgment.

It is also important to give yourself permission to grieve in your own way. There is no "right" way to mourn a miscarriage. Some women want to talk; others need silence. Some write letters, pray, journal, or create memorials; others grieve quietly in their hearts. Allow yourself grace. Grief is not a lack of faith, it is love responding honestly to loss.

TIPS FOR COPING AFTER A MISCARRIAGE

- *Name the loss.*

It is important that you do not minimize the loss to make others comfortable. Naming the loss is a necessary part of your healing. You didn't just lose a pregnancy; you lost a person, a child whom you loved. Give him or her a name if you wish but acknowledge that you lost someone you loved. Grief does not require permission from others to be real. If it mattered to you, it mattered-full stop.

- **Give yourself permission to grieve.**

As I mentioned earlier, grief is never a straight line and it may not be fully understood by many. There is no timetable for grief, no spiritual shortcut that erases sorrow overnight. The best way to get over it is to go through it. As a woman of faith, you may feel pressure to "be strong," to quote scripture quickly, or to move on before your heart is ready. But scripture reminds us that there is "a time to weep" (Ecclesiastes 3:4). God is not offended by your tears; He is near to you.

- **Know Your Triggers.**

Baby showers, due dates, pregnant mothers, newborn babies, sounds, smells, sights—triggers are things that spark a memory of your loss or stimulate certain emotions associated with your loss. Bear in mind that as you heal, you are priority. It is okay to say no to certain events if they may be triggering. Once you identify a trigger bear that in mind. If you start to react emotionally to a trigger, acknowledge it, process what is happening to you and why, then use one of your outlets or coping mechanisms to ground yourself. Remember you can experience your emotions without being overtaken or controlled by them.

- ***Find Your Outlets.***

Identify the people and the ways that you can express your emotions. Who are your inner circle people? Find them and don't be afraid to lean on them for a while. Suppressed emotions lead to toxic mindsets and behaviours. Get therapy if you need to; don't allow yourself to suffer in silence.

- ***Know Your Coping Strategies.***

What do you normally do on a very bad day or if you are in a low place and want to start feeling better? What strategies do you use to cope with difficult moments. These usually work as you are trying to cope after losing a baby. Make a list of your usual healthy coping strategies and use them to help you through this time. Some of my coping strategies were writing, listening to good music, watching a funny movie, talking with a down-to-earth friend, colouring, reading singing, going to the beach, visiting a rural community.

- ***Maintain Normalcy***

While not ignoring or denying your grieve, try to maintain as close to a normal routine as possible based on what you are dealing with. You may be given time off from work but try to do at least a few thing you normally do on a daily basis. This helps to guard your mental health.

- ***Practise Self Care***

Although this may be the farthest thing from your mind right now, be deliberate about taking care of you. Take baths, groom yourself, wear light or bright coloured clothing, practice walking or some other activity you used to enjoy. Read books that will empower you and help you heal. Two books that helped me greatly were: *It's Okay Not to Be Okay Right Now* by Mark D. Lerner PhD. and *Learning to Tell Myself the Truth*, by William Backus. I also recommend, *Grace in the Waiting* by Yetunda Dixon.

- ***Prayer, Worship and Word.***

Never underestimate the power of fellowship with God. It is the kingdom recipe for inner healing. Prayer maintains connection with God. Worship increases intimacy with God and the Word reveals the heart of God. These three disciplines of reading the word of God, worshipping God and communicating with God are absolute non-negotiables for the child of God. Much like a good multi-vitamin, this combination may not show immediate visible signs of impact but over time your spiritual immune system will be fortified and your walk with God is being strengthened. In spite of how you feel, always take your spiritual multi-vitamin-Prayer, Worship and Word. The effects over time will be evident to all.

CREATING A COPING TOOLKIT FOR YOUR HEALING JOURNEY

As part of your healing, it can be helpful to intentionally create a **coping toolkit**—a collection of practices, supports, and reminders that anchor you during difficult moments. This toolkit is personal and may evolve over time.

Your coping toolkit might include:

- **Emotional outlets** such as journaling, prayer writing, voice notes, or creative expression.
- **Spiritual anchors** like scriptures, worship music, affirmations, or reminders of God's promises when words fail.
- **Safe people** you can reach out to when grief resurfaces - those who respect your pace and your process.
- **Body-based care**, including rest, manageable exercise, nourishing food, deep breathing, or medical follow-up when needed.
- **Boundaries**, giving yourself permission to decline events, conversations, or timelines that feel overwhelming.
- **Professional support**, such as counselling, especially if feelings of sadness, anxiety, or numbness persist or intensify.

Healing after miscarriage is not about erasing pain; it is about integrating loss into your story in a way that allows life to continue with meaning. Over time, many women discover that while the loss remains sacred and tender, it also births compassion, resilience, and a deeper awareness of God's sustaining presence.

The burden lifting God sees you; he hears you; he will help you. In one of my journal entries, I wrote about how low I felt and I beseeched God to send help to me that day. While at work, Pastor Greenland called to say he must see me that day. He and Pastor Mpaji came and spoke with me and ministered to me in a profound way.

God had heard my cry and He hears yours too. Psalm 34 vs. 18 declares, *"The Lord is close to the broken-hearted and saves those who are crushed in spirit."* I can testify that that verse is true. God was near to me; I could feel him carrying me through that season and deep down I knew that in spite of the pain, I would come through the fire as pure gold.

You are not broken beyond repair. Your body is not your enemy. Your story is still unfolding. And even here—especially here—God is at work, holding every tear and redeeming what feels unbearable. He sees you.

Chapter 7

LIVING AFTER DYING-SUSTAINED IN THE DESERT

You may be wondering what I mean by living after dying. There are some experiences we have in this life that have the capacity to shut us down emotionally because of how traumatic they were. When we find ourselves in such situations we are actually at a critical crossroad where we must decide whether to continue our physical existence while remaining emotionally dead or to persevere at fully living again. Living after dying means accepting the tragedy as a part of your story that cannot be erased but choosing not to dwell at that place of pain for the rest of your life but rather with each new sunrise you rise and try to live again and eventually rise above the tragedy. It took much effort and I could not do it alone. God in his sovereignty sustained me in the desert.

THE RETURN TO REGULAR DUTIES

I recall the first time Winston and I returned to church after the miscarriage. Everyone by then was aware of what had happened and I was very apprehensive about how I would react to those who would offer hugs, words of comfort, or ask me questions. Church was packed that Sunday; I used the rear entrance to get to the platform where leaders and choir members sat. That felt safe enough and I made it through the service without crying. When it ended, I headed for the back door again but came face to face with one of the deacons who asked, "How is it going?" I felt my eyes burning and I knew what was about to happen. He hugged me and offered reassurance which actually helped as I fought to hold back the tears. I tried to get to our car quickly to avoid more conversations. To the few persons that got to me, I responded with a smile and a thank you where appropriate but chose not to engage in going over the details of what had happened with anyone that day.

Understand this, whatever trauma you have been through is your story to tell or not to tell. It is your choice. You choose who to relate it to, when to speak about it and for how long. You are not obligated to relive the trauma to satisfy people's curiosity. You are obligated to do what is best for your mental and emotional health. Self-awareness is important. Talking about the incident helps some individuals to heal faster; for others repeating the story causes more pain than relief. Do what's best for you but remember it is your story, you choose who to tell it to. It is absolutely okay to say "I prefer not to talk about that right now" and not feel guilty about it. My first choir practice following the loss was a very interesting experience as well. I was a lead singer on the choir and the director informed us that I would be leading the song, The Anchor Holds" for the coming Sunday. It was a song I knew well but this time I didn't feel like I could be the lead singer. The choir started and it got to the point where I should sing my solo. I tried but no word or sound came from my mouth. The choir director looked at me in disbelief.

"Sing Sister Megan you know the song!" "I can't." I replied softly as I felt myself breaking inside. "Why not? You know the song!" she responded.

I sat there looking at her until she decided to lead it but encouraged me to be ready for the second round. As they sang, I played over the words in my head for my verse and wondered if this lady was for real! But then maybe she just did not understand how hard it was for me a month after holding Samuel's lifeless body to hold a microphone and sing these words:

"I've had visions. I've had dreams. I've even held them in my hands. But I never knew those dreams could slip right through, like they were only grains of sand." I was not ready; I could not sing it and I knew that so again, when it was my turn to sing I told her I could not. She was not amused and went into a sort of mini lecture about people needing to be willing to sing and cooperate on the choir. Eventually I asked to be excused, went to the car and cried.

I still do not know if anyone explained to her why I could not handle the song that day but in that moment I realised that many people misunderstand and minimize the pain of losing a child in pregnancy. I also realised that as Christians we sometimes see one another as super humans who immediately bounce back after every situation, no matter how painful it was. That song was probably chosen by her with the good intention of using my story as a testimony, but the testimony was not yet fully formed in me. Timing is critical in all things. A good thing done at the wrong time can become a bad thing. That night I left choir practice feeling like my wound had been ripped open and punctured in several places all over again. I chose not to be angry for too long. I just knew I could not assume that everyone would understand.

My return to work at the Bible school office and to my graduate school were not as eventful as returning to church because individuals were more sensitive and I was not bombarded with questions or too much sympathy. For the most part everything seemed normal. I cried on the first day for each though, because of the vivid memories that came to mind when I returned. Thoughts like: "The last time you were here you were pregnant." By then I had decided to cry when I needed to so I allowed the tears to flow by pulling away by myself for a few minutes then I would square my shoulders and get on with what I had to do.

Healing from a miscarriage is a process and a key to riding through that process is to be able to listen to your emotions and express those emotions responsibly and in a way that is best for you. As I kept showing up for church, work and school it became more manageable to function productively in each space.

God continued to watch over His word in my life through various methods. He provided sustenance in the wilderness. Just like He provided manna in the wilderness for the Israelites enroute to the Promised Land, so He provided manna for my faith as I learned to believe again that He would do what He said He would do in my life.

SUSTAINED THROUGH THE WORD

There are two Greek words used for the Word of God in the Bible. 'Logos' refers to the whole infallible written word of God. Logos also refers to Jesus as the Living Word. Rhema refers to a word that is spoken-an utterance. A 'rhema' is a word or portion of scripture that the Holy Spirit brings to our attention that applies to a current situation or need.

I was an avid reader of the Logos and thankfully there were several times that I received a Rhema word from God that would reassure me that God would deliver on His word. Some I elaborated on in Chapter 4, but he added more. More strength was needed because the journey was great. May your faith be reignited as you read the ones I share here:

Habakkuk 2: 2-3 (NKJV)

²And the LORD answered me, and said, Write the vision, and make it plain upon tables, that he may run that readeth it.

³ **For the vision is yet for an appointed time, but at the end it shall speak, and not lie: though it tarry, wait for it; because it will surely come**, it will not tarry.

Isaiah 40: 5 (NKJV)

"The glory of the LORD shall be revealed, and all flesh shall see *it* together; **For the mouth of the LORD has spoken."**

Isaiah 43: 19 (NKJV)

"Behold, **I will do a new thing**, now it shall spring forth; Shall you not know it? I will even make a road in the wilderness and rivers in the desert."

1 Samuel 1- Hannah's Testimony (NKJV)

¹Now there was a certain man of Ramathaim Zophim, of the mountains of Ephraim, and his name was Elkanah the son of Jeroham, the son of Elihu, the son of Tohu, the son of Zuph, an Ephraimite. ² And he had two wives: the name of one was Hannah, and the name of the other Peninnah. Peninnah had children, but Hannah had no children. ³ This man went up from his city yearly to worship and sacrifice to the LORD of hosts in Shiloh. Also the two sons of Eli, Hophni and Phinehas, the priests of the LORD, *were*

there. ⁴And whenever the time came for Elkanah to make an offering, he would give portions to Peninnah his wife and to all her sons and daughters. ⁵But to Hannah he would give a double portion, for he loved Hannah, although the LORD had closed her womb. ⁶And her rival also provoked her severely, to make her miserable, because the LORD had closed her womb. ⁷So it was, year by year, when she went up to the house of the LORD, that she provoked her; therefore she wept and did not eat.

Then Elkanah her husband said to her, "Hannah, why do you weep? Why do you not eat? And why is your heart grieved? Am I not better to you than ten sons?"

⁹So Hannah arose after they had finished eating and drinking in Shiloh. Now Eli the priest was sitting on the seat by the doorpost of the tabernacle of the LORD. ¹⁰And she was in bitterness of soul, and prayed to the LORD and wept in anguish. ¹¹Then she made a vow and said, "O LORD of hosts, if You will indeed look on the affliction of Your maidservant and remember me, and not forget Your maidservant, but will give Your maidservant a male child, then I will give him to the LORD all the days of his life, and no razor shall come upon his head."

¹²And it happened, as she continued praying before the LORD, that Eli watched her mouth. ¹³Now Hannah spoke in her heart; only her lips moved, but her voice was not heard.

Therefore, Eli thought she was drunk. ¹⁴So Eli said to her, "How long will you be drunk? Put your wine away from you!"

¹⁵But Hannah answered and said, "No, my lord, I am a woman of sorrowful spirit. I have drunk neither wine nor intoxicating drink, but have poured out my soul before the LORD. ¹⁶Do not consider

your maidservant a wicked[c] woman, for out of the abundance of my complaint and grief I have spoken until now."

[17] Then Eli answered and said, "Go in peace, and the God of Israel grant your petition which you have asked of Him."
[18] And she said, "Let your maidservant find favour in your sight." So the woman went her way and ate, and her face was no longer _sad._

[19] Then they rose early in the morning and worshiped before the LORD, and returned and came to their house at Ramah. **And Elkanah knew Hannah his wife, and the LORD remembered her. [20] So it came to pass in the process of time that Hannah conceived and bore a son, and called his name [f]Samuel, _saying,_ "Because I have asked for him from the LORD."**

[21] Now the man Elkanah and all his house went up to offer to the LORD the yearly sacrifice and his vow. [22] But Hannah did not go up, for she said to her husband, "Not until the child is weaned; then I will take him, that he may appear before the LORD and remain there forever."

[23] So Elkanah her husband said to her, "Do what seems best to you; wait until you have weaned him. Only let the LORD establish His word." Then the woman stayed and nursed her son until she had weaned him.

[24] Now when she had weaned him, she took him up with her, with three bulls, one ephah of flour, and a skin of wine, and brought him to the house of the LORD in Shiloh. And the child was young. [25] Then they slaughtered a bull, and brought the child to Eli. [26] And she said, "O my lord! As your soul lives, my

lord, I am the woman who stood by you here, praying to the LORD. ²⁷ **For this child I prayed, and the LORD has granted me my petition which I asked of Him.** ²⁸ Therefore I also have lent him to the LORD; as long as he lives he shall be ᶦlent to the LORD." So they worshiped the LORD there."

Psalm 3- He is the lifter of my head (NKJV)

¹LORD, how they have increased who trouble me!
Many are they who rise up against me.
² Many are they who say of me,
"There is no help for him in God." *Selah*
³ **But You, O LORD, *are* a shield for me,
My glory and the One who lifts up my head.**
⁴ I cried to the LORD with my voice,
And He heard me from His holy hill. *Selah*
⁵ I lay down and slept;
I awoke, for the LORD sustained me.
⁶ I will not be afraid of ten thousands of people
Who have set themselves against me all around.
⁷ Arise, O LORD; Save me, O my God!
For You have struck all my enemies on the cheekbone;
You have broken the teeth of the ungodly.
⁸ Salvation belongs to the LORD.
Your blessing is upon Your people.

2 Chronicles 20: 20 (NKJV)

"So they rose early in the morning and went out into the Wilderness of Tekoa; and as they went out, Jehoshaphat stood and said, "Hear me, O Judah and you inhabitants of Jerusalem: **Believe in the LORD your God, and you shall be established; believe His prophets, and you shall prosper."**

Luke 1: 38 (NLT)

Mary responded, "I am the Lord's servant. **May everything you have said about me come true."** And then the angel left her.

Psalm 113: 9 (MSG)

"He gives a home to the woman who could not give birth and makes her the mother of children. Praise the Lord!" (New Living Translation)

"He gives childless couples a family, **gives them joy as the parents of children.** Hallelujah!"

SUSTAINED THROUGH SERVING WHILE WAITING

Proverbs 11:25 states: *"The generous soul will be made rich, and he who waters will also be watered himself."*

Just about a month after losing Baby Samuel, my ministerial application was approved. The official ordination ceremony was set to take place in May 2008 during a Parish Convention of the Church of God of Prophecy. I struggled with whether to accept the position as I was still in the healing process and I was not sure how much I had to offer at the time.

As I pondered, my mind went back to approximately four years prior, to the beginning of one of my most impactful areas of ministry. One afternoon while at home I felt led to start a Teens Ministry at the church I attended. It was to be named Kingdom Teenz. My husband and I obeyed God and within a few months we had over 20 teenagers under our care and the full blessing of our pastor to teach and mentor them. I still smile when I remember that group of teens. They became our children, we learned so much from them and they grew in God. Sometimes God will challenge you to give more than you think you have in the same area in which you are waiting for him to work a miracle for you, and as you obey he will give you the grace and the anointing to do what he asks and He will be glorified.

We had Bible studies, prayer and fasting, picnics, road trips, pyjama parties with these teens. We counselled and prayed with them, visited their homes, met with their parents, challenged them to do well in school. We spent two days on the road searching for one of them who had run away from home due to depression - thank God she was found. Kingdom Teenz was a holistic ministry that started out of obedience and it transformed us. I remember taking one of the teens to my general practitioner because she wasn't feeling well. We had her and her one-year-old baby sister over for a few days. Can you imagine me taking care of a one year old while praying for a child of my own? As I sat in the doctor's office she said to me, "God will bless you with children. He has to! When I look at what you do for other people's children I know He must bless you."

Reflecting on the impact of the Kingdom Teenz programme led to my decision to give God another yes; to move in obedience and answer the call to ministry. The call was bigger than my current circumstance and I felt compelled to yield.

I was formally licensed as a Minister of the Gospel on March 30, 2008. As I knelt with the other new ministers and was prayed for by the Parish Overseer, tears streamed down my face. It was a bitter-sweet experience. God alone knew what I was feeling inside but I stuck with my decision to say yes to the call.

Serving others had become my safe place and one of my greatest sources of joy for the last nine years. It brought much fulfilment to me and took my eyes off my own problems. I had served in the Youth Ministry, Christian Education and in the Camping Ministry of the church at the local, parish and national levels. At this point, I would continue to serve God and trust him with the other areas of my life. Serving God and his people had sustained me in the wilderness of waiting. I was not about to walk away now.

SUSTAINED THROUGH DIVINE CONNECTIONS & PROPHETIC ENCOUNTERS

I want to reiterate that when God intends to do big things in your life, He will often create divine connections as well as prophetic encounters. These often come in the guise of ministers, friends or associates and it is usually in retrospect that we recognise the hand of God in those happenings. Here I describe more of the divine connections that God made during this period of my wilderness experience. Persons sent to ensure that my faith would not wane and to give instructions that would activate the manifestation of the promises He had made.

Earlier in the journey the encounters were to influence change in my thinking, my speaking and my behaviour. At this point, the encounters were for manifestation of promise. I had no idea at the time that this was so, but I thank God I did not miss them. May you not miss your divine connections and prophetic encounters in this season of your life.

Starting May 2008 - Rev. Cecelia Bailey

Rev. Cecelia Bailey was my pastor. She was a stalwart in the faith who had served in ministry for decades and truly believed that there was absolutely nothing impossible with God. Following the miscarriage, she would have three words to say in almost every conversation with me - 'Baby Must Come'. Sometimes no one else would hear her but me, but at other times it came out with force and power in spite of who was around me. Proverbs 18 vs. 21 states that death and life are in the power of the tongue. Rev. Bailey knew the authority she carried as our spiritual covering and she used it to declare 'BABY MUST COME'. Even when to us, it felt embarrassing, she would look me in the eyes and declare again: "Baby must come." I thank God for her boldness and determination in agreeing with that which God had revealed to her and releasing that word continuously over our lives. Now I know it was a divinely orchestrated prophetic utterance.

August 2008 - Pastor Charles Mpaji

Through Pastor Greenland, I had the privilege of meeting a man of God from Uganda, Africa-Pastor Charles Mpaji. He was visiting Jamaica for the first time and Pastor Greenland invited us out to dinner with Pastor Mpaji, his wife and himself one Friday night in April. This was just about two months after the miscarriage and probably our first time going out like that since it happened. I tried my best to act as normal as possible but every smile took a lot out of me. When we got back to our gate just before we went inside Pastor Greenland told Pastor Mpaji about the miscarriage and how it had affected us. He sympathized but spoke with quiet confidence as he assured us that everything would be fine and that God would move on our behalf.

The day before he returned to Uganda, Pastor Mpaji along with Pastor Greenland came to visit us, and Winston cooked up a delicious Jamaican meal. It was refreshing, having both men of God dine with us. Pastor Mpaji wanted to pray with us before leaving and as I sat and waited for him to start I could hear my heart saying 'no more word please I am fine." Yes, that's where I was. I had gotten so many prophecies. I was at the point where manifestation is what I longed for. I thank God that he sees beyond what we think we need to what we truly need.

I was lost in my thoughts as Pastor Mpaji prayed thinking about all I had been through. "I see a daughter in your womb." Those words jolted me back to reality. What did he just say? And he said it with confident calmness. "It's a girl child that you will carry and it will be well. She will be here the next time I visit Jamaica." He had not said much but it was the most specific message I had received so far. I don't think either of us really knew how to respond. My eyes filled with tears and I heard my husband say "Amen".

October 2008 - Rev. Anthony

One day while working at the church office where I was serving as Administrative Assistant for the Bible School my phone rang. It was Rev. Anthony calling. I had grown to trust him as he had been there for more than 15 years of my life as a steady voice of wisdom and guidance. He was away in England but said he felt led to call and pray with me because it was 'time for a change'. I got no opportunity to tell him about my doubtful thoughts because he went straight into prayer and ministry.

It was an intense time of praying and it seems God had locked down my office because for the entire time that he was praying, no one came inside. As he prayed, I felt a heat in my womb moving from one side to the next…it was like liquid fire! I had no idea what God was doing but I knew something was happening inside my body. For about 20 minutes after he had ended the call I just sat there in awe, tears streaming down my face. God had walked into that room because of the obedience of one of his sons. It was so profound that it felt sacred and the only person I told about that call at the time was my husband when I got home.

January 2009 - Pastor Wade

One weekday morning while I was at work at the church office, Pastor Wade came to see me. He was walking by the building and God instructed him to stop and check to see how I was doing. This was the same pastor who had prophesied that even the trees on my property would be fruitful. I was happy for the opportunity to speak with someone I trusted about how I had been feeling.

After listening to me for a while he just started chuckling. To be honest I was a bit puzzled because in my opinion what I was going through was no laughing matter.

"Megan, Megan," he said softly, "If you could see what I am seeing now, you would be laughing too. Your answered prayer is so much closer than you know." I tried to digest what the man of God was saying but it was hard because I feared being disappointed all over again. I was one month away from the first anniversary of Baby Samuel's passing, and it felt like yesterday. Nevertheless, I knew Pastor Wade had a history of accuracy in the prophetic and so deep inside I felt that flicker of hope. He prayed with me before he left and reassured me that God was about to move in a big way.

January 2009 - Ivan Fast

Brother Ivan was a youth leader that Ugandan Pastor Mpaji had connected me with. The aim was to create connections between the youths in both our churches. That was another divine connection. Ivan could be described as a young man who was 'cooked in prayer'. Praying was like oxygen to him. It seemed he literally could not live without praying. Prior to meeting Ivan I thought that my prayer life was good but I soon realised that I was nowhere near where I should have been! Ivan would wake up at 3 a.m. daily to pray. Then he would walk to his church for 5 a.m. prayer before leaving for work and when he got home in the nights, he would again spend much time in prayer.

As we spoke and made plans for our youths, Ivan learned of my battle with barrenness and the miscarriages I had had. He started asking if I believed God could change things and give me a child. At first, I said I hoped so but eventually I started saying yes. In January 2009, Ivan challenged me to join him on a three-day fast as he sensed God wanted to bless my womb. I agreed and we started the fast. My plan was to eat at the end of each day. At the end of Day 1 when Ivan called for us to pray, he commented that we had just two more days to go. I asked, "So you have not eaten?" Ivan was somewhat shocked. He told me he was willing to make that sacrifice and I should not let him want the miracle more than I did. Ouch!

I asked God for strength and buckled up for the next 48 hours water fast. I was determined that I could not let Ivan want my miracle more than I did. I remember vividly on the third day when we were praying by phone, Ivan said, "I heard God say - it is done. What you desired is now granted." He had such a confidence in his voice that it was literally contagious and I too felt hope - the flicker of hope had become a flame. I felt like the matter was settled once and for all.

January 2009 -Bishop Senior

There was a parish fasting service scheduled to be held at my local church on the last Wednesday of January 2009. I was on leave from work and as a parish youth leader I made plans to be there. The speaker was the Parish Overseer, Bishop R. Senior. The anointing was rich, and he was very deliberate about praying for deliverance, healing and miracles that day. Being a member of the praise team, I was sitting on the platform close to my pastor, Rev. Bailey. I wrote a note to her, asking her to pray for me that on that day God would remember me like he remembered Hannah. She read the note and looked across at me. My eyes watered, my heart was desperate for a miracle. She beckoned to me and I went and stooped beside her chair.

"Can I show this to the overseer?" she asked. I was a very private person but at that point I felt like I no longer cared about what people might think. There comes a point when you are so hungry for God to move in your life that you really care little what people will think or say. "Yes Pastor." I replied and returned to my seat as she got up and moved towards the overseer.

"Minister Hylton," I heard him say. I stood up and went to him at the altar. He had my note in his hand and asked the church to stand with him as it was time for my miracle. He spoke about the power of the prophetic word and asked some women from my church to come and stand with me charging them not to stop praying until this word for a baby is manifested. He prayed. The women prayed. The church prayed. It was like one voice in unison going up to God. I wept as I stood there-only God knew how desperate I was. At the end of the prayer Bishop said, "It is done, now go and do what you are supposed to do." I obeyed.

As you journey through your wilderness experience, pray that you will not miss your divine connections. God says he will watch over His word to perform it and many times he uses his children here on earth to water that word for it to bring forth fruit. Be careful not to disconnect from those whom God is trying to connect you with while you wait. He often shows up through men and women who are available to be used by Him.

Sitting under the tutelage of my spiritual father Apostle Dr. Courtney McLean, in prophetic school has opened my eyes to many things. I did not know him then but most of what I experienced during the ten-year journey to motherhood, I now understand at another level. God was in my story. Even in the moments when I felt alone, he was there. He always sent a word, He always did something to remind me that He cannot lie. He sustained me in the wilderness. God is sovereign and even in your darkest moments He never takes His eyes off you.

Can you identify God in your story? I am sure He is there, working things together for your good. There is no place you can go where he cannot reach you. Psalm 139 vs. 7-12 says it beautifully:

"[7]Where can I go from your Spirit?
    Where can I flee from your presence?
[8] If I go up to the heavens, you are there;
    if I make my bed in the depths, you are there.
[9] If I rise on the wings of the dawn,
    if I settle on the far side of the sea,
[10] even there your hand will guide me,
    your right hand will hold me fast.
[11] If I say, "Surely the darkness will hide me
    and the light become night around me,"
[12] even the darkness will not be dark to you;

the night will shine like the day,
for darkness is as light to you."

God is in your story. May your eyes be opened to see Him.

Wilderness Treasures:

- **Don't miss your divine connections.**

Be careful not to disconnect from those whom God is trying to connect you with while you wait. He often shows up through men and women who are available to be used by Him.

- **Feed on the Word of God.**

The Word of God is a wellspring of inner strength and fortitude. Never stop drawing from the well.

- **Maintain your passion.**

Don't allow someone else to want your miracle more than you do. Be passionate about seeking God for answered prayer.

Luke 21 vs. 13

"And it shall turn
to
You for a
Testimony."

IT WILL TURN INTO A TESTIMONY

Chapter 8

FAITH MANIFESTED – THE TURNING POINT

One morning a few weeks later, I had to go to work at the church office but I did not feel well at all. It had been several days since I was feeling this way but experience had taught me to be cautiously optimistic. I made my way to work nonetheless but decided to take the all too familiar trek to the pharmacy nearby during lunch time. I told no one at work where I was going and why, just in case the pregnancy test was negative-again.

As soon as I returned to the office I took the test. Three minutes felt like forever…I dreaded looking at it but when I did I was at a loss for words…two lines! Wait, two lines? What? Two lines! Two lines meant that I was pregnant. I could feel my heart pounding against my chest and I sat to let it sink in.

Eventually I got up and looked again. I didn't want to tell hubby the news by phone so the next best person would be to call my gynaecologist. As the receptionist answered and I identified myself she said, "Oh, Mrs. Hylton, we were trying to reach you. We just got back some test results and Dr. Mitchell wants you to come in soon to discuss them because there are some concerns."

"Concerns?" I replied. "Well, I am calling because I just got a positive result on a pregnancy test!" "What! That's great! Let me get Dr. Mitchell." I waited anxiously to hear my doctor's voice. "Hi Megan, how are you?" Dr Mitchell asked. I quickly told her what had just happened. She sounded as excited as I was and told me to come in as soon as possible to see her. As I ended the call it felt like a dream. Was it beginning to turn? Was my story changing? Was this the beginning of answered prayers?

Needless to say, as soon as Winston arrived to pick me up that afternoon I told him everything. I could see the joy on his face but I could also see that he was being cautiously optimistic. We made arrangements to see Dr. Mitchell in a few days time and the pregnancy was confirmed. She was not about to take any chances and reassured us that together we would do all we needed to in order get this baby here safe and sound. I was placed on folic acid and sent to do my first ultrasound procedure.

The brain is an amazing organ, it makes imprints of significant experiences and the emotions we had with them. As I lay on the bed waiting for the ultrasound to begin, I could hear my heartbeat echo through the quiet room. The last time I did this procedure the news was not good. Thankfully, all went well and I breathed a sigh of relief as the doctor emphasized that 'everything looked perfect'. I asked them to print the images and as I collected them I felt an unusual warmth inside.

At our next visit, Dr. Mitchell explained that based on the previous miscarriages, I would need to do a minor procedure to insert a cerclage at about 12-14 weeks of pregnancy. A cerclage is a stitch placed at the neck of the womb to prevent early opening of the cervix and consequently premature birth and possible death of the foetus. Though a bit nerve wracking, the procedure went well and was followed by two weeks of bed rest and six months of no heavy lifting, or heavy housework and no sex! God granted grace for the journey. We were both willing to do our part in bringing little Hylton home—lol.

Every day over the next 8 months was a gift that Winston and I had to treasure. The mission was clear, ensuring all was done within our power to have a healthy baby at the end of this period. Doctor's visits were not missed; her instructions were taken seriously. Prayer and declarations were not optional and self-care was priority. Initially, we were very selective of the persons who were made aware of the baby on board.

Each day I would lay my hands on my womb and again ask God to take us through this. As time progressed and the secret became public, excitement grew among our relatives, friends and church family. God had answered prayers and things were heading in the right direction.

When I began to feel the baby moving it felt surreal! I was living what I had prayed for. I was still in school pursuing my Master's Degree in Counselling Psychology. I was on the final leg but that meant more assignments and preparation for the dreaded comprehensive examination. I wasn't sure I wanted to push myself so hard, so I made an appointment with the Director for the program and was approved to do my Comprehensive exam in the next year, following the birth of my baby. This would mean that most of my batchmates would graduate ahead of me but I was willing to sacrifice that rather than to put this pregnancy at risk.

NEW CHAPTER

I want you to understand that when God promises you something big and begins to activate that promise, the enemy will not just sit back and watch you step into your blessing. Like a snake whose head has been severed he will give one last fight flashing his body vigorously still trying to cause harm to its target. For us as covenant sons and daughters of God we are assured that God is always fighting for us and the fight is fixed in our favour. Even when the enemy gives a last flash the angels of the Lord encamp round about them that fear God and delivers them.

I was now eight months pregnant and I had an appointment with Dr. Mitchell in Kingston. The plan was to take public transportation to meet my husband in Half-Way-Tree and then he would drive me up to the University Hospital. I left home a little late and decided to take a taxi instead of a bus. Upon approaching the taxi-stand, several drivers approached me, hungry for another passenger so they could be on their way. I scanned the area and saw a taxi that was almost full and decided to take that one. Somehow though, my eyes zoomed in on the license plate and I realized it was not a licensed public passenger vehicle but a 'robot taxi' as the unlicensed taxis are called in Jamaica. Deep inside I felt like Holy Spirit was prompting me not to board the car. I went in anyway.

About fifteen minutes into our journey, the driver stopped for a passenger to get out and I heard Holy Spirit say, "Get out here." I convinced myself that it was my mind. Getting off there would mean taking a bus to Half-Way-Tree and I was already late. As we drove off I felt a very uneasy feeling and again at the next stop I felt like getting out of the car. Looking back, I realise God was speaking to me but I perceived Him not.

At the next major intersection about 3 minutes away I heard the driver comment that the Transport Authority had 'spotted' him. Within seconds he turned off his route and began driving like a madman through a community, trying to get away from his pursuers - police and Transport Authority personnel. The passengers were screaming, begging him to stop. I was shouting, "Driver I am pregnant!" He was seemingly deaf to all our pleas as he kept going. I prayed for mercy because I realised then what God had been trying to protect me from.

The Transport Authority vehicles were closing in on us, and I was praying they wouldn't start shooting at the vehicle. I begged God to have mercy on my baby; we had come too far now for another tragedy. Suddenly, I saw one of their vans speed past us and block the vehicle I was in; a police car drove up on the right as they tried to pin him in. The passengers at the back opened their doors and scampered out as the car came to a sudden stop. I opened my door at the front and put my left foot outside. As soon as I stood up, I felt the car start reversing. As I was falling backwards, I saw a policeman point his gun towards the driver's chest and he pressed the brake. I fell to the ground and I felt the hot wheel touch my right leg. Had the police not put the gun on him that car would have run over my leg.

I looked up and saw two police officers standing nearby. We were on the side of a major thoroughfare. I shouted, "Officer I am pregnant. Help me!" That sparked an immediate response from both men. They helped me up and began shooting questions at me rapidly. "Are you feeling any pain? Can you feel the baby moving? Where is your doctor located?" Soon I was in a police car, sirens blaring, heading to the emergency room at the University Hospital of the West Indies (UHWI), where I was registered for delivery. Dr Mitchell and Winston had been informed and the staff at UHWI were supposedly awaiting my arrival. Tears filled my eyes, this was surreal. Obviously, I had walked right into a trap of the enemy. Would my baby survive? My mind went away from all that was happening around me as the thought of losing another baby seemed unfathomable. I was jolted back into reality as the wound on my leg from the hot car wheel burned, the police in the passenger seat was on the phone explaining to someone what had happened. The one driving began to caution me against taking these 'robot' taxis; I felt terrible because, yes, the Holy Spirit had warned me.

Understand that in spite of the journey you are on He promises to walk alongside us and he will or I dare say he always seeks to steer us away from danger. The critical question is, "Are our ears open to hear Him and if we hear Him, will we obey? In your journey of faith be intentional about hearing and obeying God-even His simplest commands.

When we got to the hospital, checks were made on both the baby and me and the doctors decided to admit me for the night as a precautionary measure. The baby was doing well and so was I. The next day we were discharged and I knew the enemy had lost again—God had extended mercy!

BABY SHOWER

The last trimester of this first pregnancy was the most challenging. Nobody prepared me for this! Sleeping comfortably had become a vague memory. But when you have waited ten years for this, nothing warrants a complain. My sleepless nights were spent thanking God for His blessings, looking for baby names and wondering or more so worrying about labour.

Two of my sisters-in-law visited to the USA for the summer of 2009 and I believe they had but one mission - to go shopping for Megan's baby. Note that we had no idea what the gender of the baby was. Every ultrasound to date proved inconclusive. This little one was very private, or God was reserving some information for when the time was right. My sisters in law returned with so many gifts for baby and as I went through them reality hit me; my eyes welled with tears...God had answered our prayers! Joy filled my heart the dream was unfolding.

The baby's first set of God parents was established early. Yes, you guessed right. My friends who had brought the prophetic gifts of the baby pram, car seat and play pen were godparents. One day I was told they wanted us to come for dinner before my delivery date drew near. That wasn't strange so I complied and planned accordingly. The day came and I was ready early (quite unusual then to be honest) but Winston kept delaying and was always on his phone answering calls. I began to wonder...was something else up? Were they trying to surprise me?

Well, when I got to Denise and Junior's home, everything looked normal, there were no extra vehicles or strange faces just them, so my suspicions seemed unwarranted. I entered the house and was almost floored by a resounding SURPRISE!!!! OMG !!! There were almost 40 persons there! Familiar faces- friends, brethren and relatives, who had prayed and believed God with us. It was our Baby Shower. It was a night filled with joy, laughter and fellowship. One of my favourite songs is *"Look What The Lord Has Done"* by Nathaniel Bassey. Even though it wasn't written at the time of my story changing, it certainly captures what I experienced.

"Look what the Lord has done. Look what the Lord has done. What we've waited for has come to pass. Look what the Lord has done."

A highlight of the Baby Shower was seeing my childhood best friend and the one who had encouraged me at 13 years old to surrender to Christ, Dawn Petgrave. I had not seen her since High school years! She had moved to the United States and we lost contact but had recently reconnected by social media once in the previous year. What she shared with me that night proved to me that God had been summoning His warriors far and wide to pray me through the process and to pray the promise into reality.

DAWN'S TESTIMONY

"Some years ago, around 2008, a retired couple from my church in Orlando, Florida, asked me to drive them to Tampa to a healing crusade. To be honest, that was not my thing, but they were unable to drive themselves and so I decided to take them.

When I got to the crusade, the preacher was filled with tattoos and that threw me off (sorry, I might have judged him). So, I was more annoyed than anything else, convincing myself, this is why I don't like these kinds of gatherings.

Nonetheless, while I stood there, I could hear the Holy Spirit saying to me "Megan Angus". So, I questioned why I am hearing Megan's name. I had not seen her since high school. But it was so strong in my spirit that I needed to pray for her I couldn't shake it. So reluctantly in the atmosphere of that healing crusade, I prayed " God, bless Megan Angus".

The same night after returning from the crusade, I looked up Megan on the Hi-Five social media platform. I shared with her what happened at the crusade and she responded that she had been married for several years and was trying to conceive for a while but lost the baby she had believed for and that she and her husband were devastated. I prayed with her and encouraged her to trust God through that difficult season.

In March 2009, I returned to Jamaica. A few months later I ran into a friend who told me Megan was pregnant and they were having a baby shower for her. So of course, I showed up at the baby shower and surprised her!"

Isn't God amazing? He is a covenant keeping God. He watches over his word to perform it. When my soul was too wounded to pray, when I needed a trusted voice in my ear, God summoned Dawn and she was sensitive enough to obey and to reach out to me. The Prophetic gift in the body of Christ is real. The Holy Spirit continues to be living and active in the church. I give Jesus all the glory!

The next couple of weeks felt like eternity! One spark of light was that my final ultra-sound revealed that we were having a baby girl. We were delighted: but this was just two weeks before our due date- and almost everything was neutral in colour. I recall we went to Ammars clothes store in Kingston and picked out a beautiful pink chemise, cool and nicely embroidered-for our miracle baby girl.

I had moved to weekly visits and things were progressing nicely. I was experiencing pain occasionally and so I was told by Dr Mitchell to come in on the Tuesday before my due date for a check-up. Well, I was sent to the labour ward as she was concerned that labour had not yet started. We were taking no risks. Baby Hylton seemed very comfortable inside, no rush whatsoever. I spent the next two days waiting, no sign of labour - then on her exact due date the action started. I want to scare no one so I will reserve the details of the pain I went through. But I must share again-how God was in the room! What makes a journey of faith authentic is the undeniable presence of God each step of the way - even when you can't see Him, He is working!

On the night of October 7 while resting on the labour ward, the silence was pierced by the sound of shoes heels coming through the passage. It was Dr. Mitchell. "Megan, what are you still doing here looking so comfortable? I expected to find you on the delivery ward. I came to deliver the baby!" She smiled, "Not to worry tomorrow it is, for sure." She did her quick examinations and encouraged me to get all the rest I could because I would need it the next day.

Needless to say, I woke up excited. I had heard of labour, but it would soon be my turn. At about 1 pm I started feeling an unusual pain across my lower abdomen. It moved from left to right then eased, then came again. I had watched enough documentaries to know that I was entering labour, so I recorded the time gaps between the contractions and eventually told the nurse.

I was transferred to the labour ward and was almost traumatized by the wails and screams of judgment from many of those in active labour. All necessary preliminaries were done and labour progressed nicely with agonizing pain of course and after about 5 hours I was moved again to the delivery room. By this time, I felt like I had run a 5k marathon - I was exhausted. I had nothing left to give-and my little miracle was tired too. She had gone into cruise mode and was no longer helping me to get the job done.

"Megan," my doctor said with firm determination, "We have to get this baby out. Her heart rate is dropping. I am not coming this far to lose her. Find every strength you have left and push. If not, I am taking you into the theatre - there is the door. This baby is coming out alive tonight." I knew I had to do this but I was weak. God I need help, I thought. I started crying but the doctor encouraged me, "Don't cry put that energy in the next push. At that point a nurse who was on duty started encouraging me and praying at the same time. You can do this Megan. I am not leaving until she is here."

At that point Nurse Rosie climbed onto the side of the bed, placed both hands on my stomach and started helping me to push that baby out. With each contraction we pushed together. My husband was holding one of my hands and encouraging me to keep going. Within a few minutes, Baby Abi entered the world with a cry that announced the faithfulness of God-she was tired but healthy. It felt surreal. Tears rolled down my cheeks-God had brought us through. My miracle baby was here.

As you read these pages, let me remind you that God is true to his word. He said he is a very present help in time of trouble. He works all things together for the good of his children. That nurse was the sister-in-law of one of my closest friends and a member of a branch of the church I was a member of. She knew the journey, she knew the story and she was passionate about the birthing of the miracle. She later told me that her shift ended that day at two p.m. but when she saw me come in for delivery she felt compelled to stay and told her supervisor she would do some extra time. Dr Mitchell asked me afterwards who that nurse was because she had never seen anything like that before. That nurse, she said, was sent by God.

I didn't just write this book to tell my story; I wrote it to encourage someone who needs to know that God will not start you on a journey of faith and leave you helpless. At every step of the way, He's got you.

I slept that night because I was exhausted but everything felt fresh and new. Each time I opened eyes, I looked across at the beautiful baby girl God had given us. This time it wasn't a dream. I was living the dream.

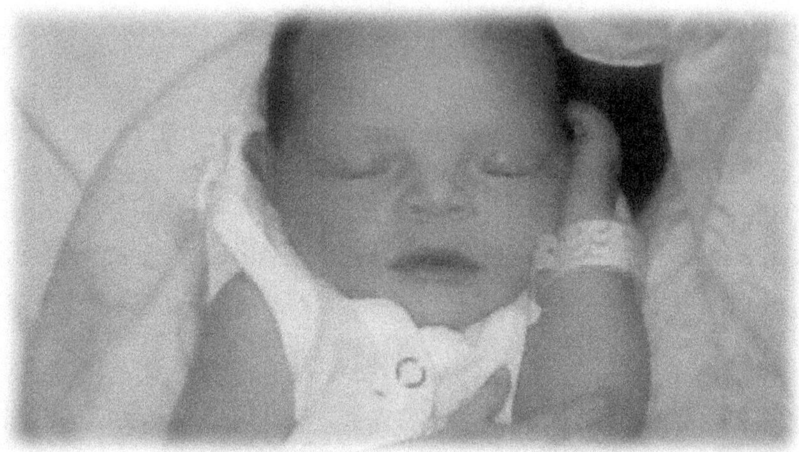

Abigail's birth was the miracle that broke years of pain and barrenness. The matter was settled. God had kept his word and I was at peace. The long years of waiting had finally given way to pure joy. I poured myself into motherhood, savouring every moment -even the tiring ones. I had no right to complain, for this child we prayed! Doctor's visits, vaccines, family gatherings, church. Life had taken on a whole new meaning; God had changed our story. The naysayers were silenced and the enemies were shocked. My favourite times were just holding her after her morning baths and singing her to sleep. I believe she also looked forward to those moments.

I was still in graduate school and so just three months after her birth I had to start the practicum leg of the journey. I remember vividly, the first day I had to leave my baby at home — torture! It felt like the longest day of my life! Eventually I adjusted to the realities of studying and motherhood. Many nights were spent completing assignments while breastfeeding but complaining was not an option. My joy was complete.

We were very deliberate and intentional about Abigail's dedication. Those who had laboured with us in prayer and faith were invited to a special dedication service and God spoke in no uncertain terms assuring us that he would give us grace to parent this gift and we should remember that he had favoured us. Abigail grew beautifully. Her personality was warm but it was clear to me she would be a deep thinker. Crying was her favourite past time and her soother was music or being taken for a ride in a vehicle. To this day she loves good music and will listen for hours and yes, she loves a good trip.

Winston and I were enjoying the parenting journey, it had been a long wait. We celebrated her first birthday with joy and she understood her assignment - stepping into her cake and squealing with delight. LOL. Having a healthy happy child felt like the crescendo of our parenting story but God had more to write. One night as I lay Abi to bed, a thought crossed my mind: "What if I had more children?" I quickly caught myself and tried to dismiss the thought but the truth is that it was strangely intriguing. I pondered it in my heart but why would I even want to go through all that tension and caution for another nine months? The desire felt extremely strong and I prayed, "If it is your will Lord, let it be so…"

Psalm 102:13

"Thou shalt arise, and have mercy upon Zion (Megan): for the time to favour her, yea, the set time, is come."

THERE IS A SET TIME OF FAVOUR FOR YOU

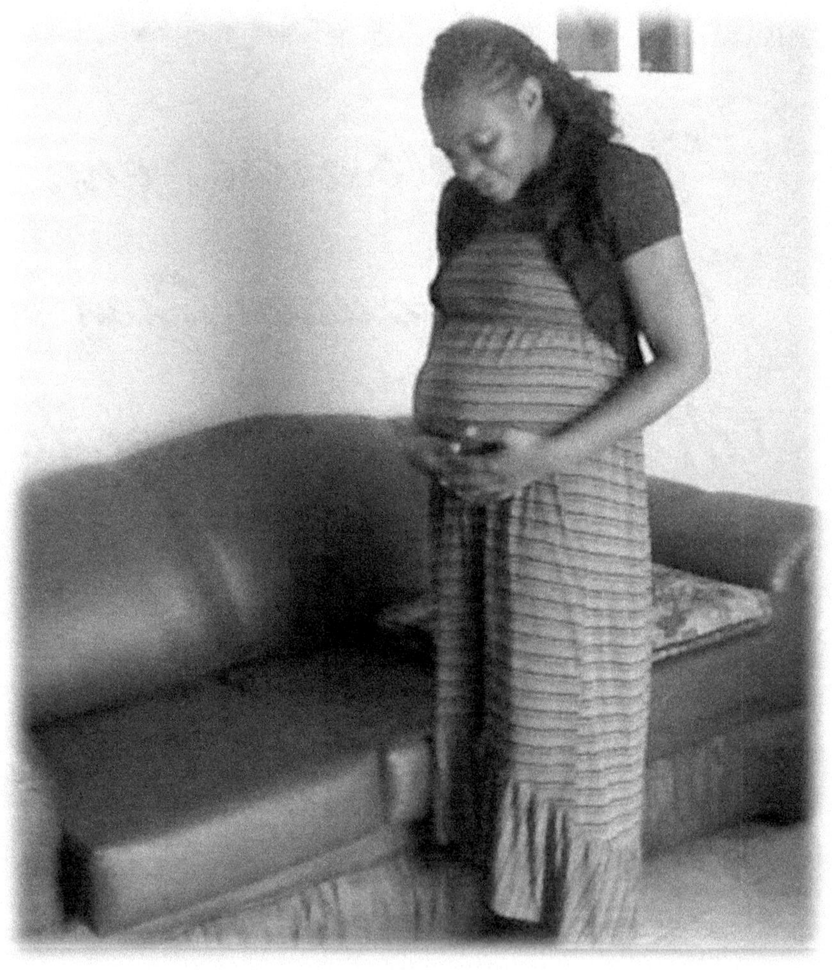

Chapter 9

GRACE MULTIPLIED

It was January 2011. I had returned to work as a teacher and was on the afternoon shift. My regular routine most mornings was to take Abigail to the nursery by taxi and then walk home and get ready to leave for work a few hours later. Her father worked in Kingston and had to leave home very early. It took me approximately 15-minutes to walk home each day -which, of course, was healthy and refreshing.

I can recall one morning though when I felt rather queasy walking home and when I finally got in, I had to sleep before getting ready for work. Over the next few days, everything felt tiring, I was sleepy, lacked energy and always wanted to stay in bed. The journey to work almost 20 miles away felt like forever. That was unlike me and I began to wonder what was happening. I was honestly too scared to even mention that I thought I was pregnant, so I stopped at a pharmacy and bought a pregnancy kit and used it early the next morning just after Winston left for work.

Two lines!!! Two lines!!! Two lines???? Whoa…my mind went blank for a few seconds. I sat in my living room trying to let it sink in-I was pregnant-again? Immediately I remembered the prophetic word I had received years ago: "You are going to be very fruitful even the trees of your land will be fruitful". Tears welled in my eyes-tears that reflected joy and anxiety-this meant the beginning of another journey of trying to have a successful pregnancy. I messaged Dr. Mitchell and gave her the news-needless to say, she was excited and told me to come in soon. The smile that lit Winston's face when I showed him the test was indescribable. God had done it again. Seriously, I felt like I just thought about it and the blessing was released! In that moment I felt like I had experienced Isaiah 65 vs 24: *"And it shall come to pass, that before they call, I will answer; and while they are yet speaking, I will hear."*

The second pregnancy went smoothly for the most part. I had to do the cerclage procedure again and all went well. One thing for sure I knew God was showing up and showing off. During our second ultrasound the sonographer commented, "This one is having a party in there!" She was doing cartwheels in my stomach! and believe me when I tell you she is the most active of all my children to this day.

At seven months pregnant, we were approached by Bishop Senior. We were selected to pastor a small rural church in St. Catherine, Jamaica. Pastoral work was not something I had aspired towards but somehow, I felt like I could give God nothing less than my yes. He had been so faithful and there was nothing too hard to give him in return. We got the blessing of our pastor and prepared for the transition.

At eight months pregnant and with Abigail being a toddler, we said yes to the call and were inaugurated as pastors. It was an unforgettable night. The support from the other leaders and ministers in the parish was overwhelming. I sat there nervous but encouraged. I wondered if I was taking on too much but I knew from an early age that my life was not my own. The anointing was rich that night and my yes was complete. God would provide the grace and He did.

Psychologists and other scientists state that babies in utero are sensitive to their environment and eventually form attachments with the persons in their family, especially those whose voices they hear often. Abigail, at almost two years old, was very excited about the baby in Mommy's tummy and would sing and speak to her, as much as she could at that age. I noticed most times the baby's movements would increase whenever Abi spoke to her.

Choosing a name for Baby # 2 was a task we had several possible names. One day while on my way home from my doctor's visit, Winston and I were talking about the possible names. I called out three and then we heard Abi in her car seat at the back saying, "Gianna, Gianna, Gianna" and looking through the window smiling. It was settled, our second girl would be named Gianna.

A few weeks later, we decided to take Abigail to my parents because my due date was approaching. It was the first time we were leaving her with anyone and it was hard. I called regularly. I missed her soooo much! After five days I could take it no longer. I told Winston I wanted to go back for Abigail because obviously Gianna was taking her own time. We went to get her on Friday evening and headed back home. We stopped at a supermarket to get some snacks. Abigail was really happy to see us and I could feel Gianna moving more since we got her sister back. While walking through the supermarket aisle I felt a very sharp pain. It was so painful I had to stop walking. It lasted a while then eased off. I proceeded to the cashier and we went home.

I was up early Saturday morning. I was very restless and went to check if the new baby's drawer was well stacked. I found myself folding and looking at her clothes, fixing things etc. I checked the play pen she would be sleeping in. Abigail and Winston were still asleep. (Note: This behaviour is called Nesting. Nesting in pregnancy refers to a strong, instinctive urge that many pregnant women experience to prepare for their baby's arrival. It usually occurs in the final weeks and days of pregnancy and for some women may be an indicator that labour is looming.

Well, that was exactly the case for me. As soon as I finished repacking the drawer and moved towards my bedroom, I felt a pain and a gush. It felt like I was smack in the middle of a Hollywood movie. "Winston!" I screamed. He jumped out of bed and found me standing frozen in the passage, water all over the floor. "Call Dr. Mitchell please" I told him. He called and told me to get ready right away. Gianna was making her entrance into the world.

To this day I am convinced the little lady had staged a one-week protest in utero. She was not about to come out unless her Abigail was home. So, the day after we brought Abi home Gianna was born. We had to leave Abi at my aunt in Kingston on the way to the hospital. Labour was long and painful but much easier than the first time. It felt like a dream. I was about to be a mother …again. God had released double for my trouble!

At dusk that Saturday evening I gave birth to our gracious gift - Gianna. Dr Mitchell smiled and commented, "I feel like you had the same baby twice! She looks just like her sister." As she lay Gianna on my chest, I finally understood what it meant to love two persons completely and uniquely, none more than the other but a full wholesome authentic love. I held her close as she wiggled slowly and I looked above my head into the eyes of my husband. We were thankful…God was speaking loudly in our lives - our story had changed again.

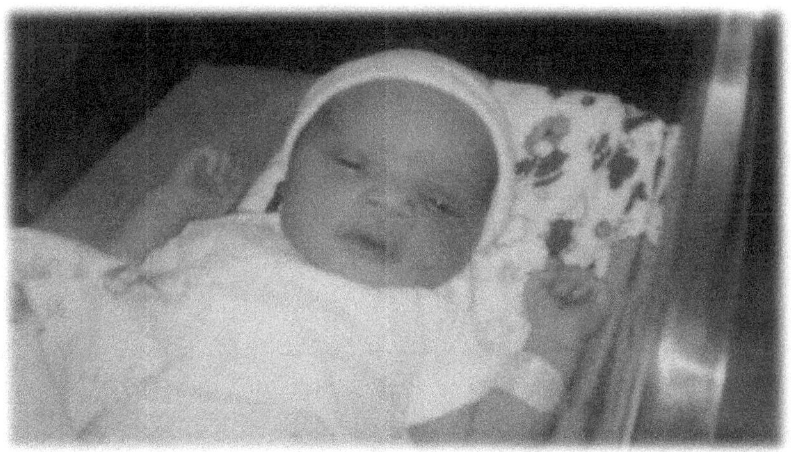

The next two weeks were exciting and tiring as I got used to being the mother of a newborn and a toddler. Little Abigail was elated to have new company. Joy filled our home and hearts but of course, the enemy was not happy with the season of manifestation. I realised one day that Gianna was not breathing well and took her back to the hospital for a check-up. We were there for hours and my patience was running thin. I began to wonder if I had made the right decision. Soon a doctor came and advised us that the baby had to be admitted as they suspected she had a chest infection. Tears welled in my eyes. There began a 1 week stay for both of us.

I was determined I would not leave her side. I slept on an uncomfortable board chair beside her bed. On the third day, they started giving her antibiotics intra venously. I had an uncomfortable feeling about all this but I was no medical doctor. At intervals I would lay hands on her and pray - asking God to intervene and to cover and deliver her from any evil plots and plans. An x-ray was done but the doctors never provided any feedback even when I asked. They seemed to have been junior doctors and just insisted that she must complete the treatment.

On the seventh morning being there, I noticed a doctor enter the ward. She carried an atmosphere of authority and there were some student doctors with her. She was moving to different beds and checking on the young patients. As she approached Gianna she said good morning to me. I was hoping to at least get a better understanding of what was happening. I responded and sat and listened as they had their discourse using medical terms I did not understand. Suddenly she looked back on Gianna's file, and said, "Why is this baby being given antibiotics? Who approved it? Let me see her x-rays." They walked away briskly with her at the lead and a few minutes later returned to where we were.

She was obviously disturbed and instructed the nurses to stop the medication right away because she had no need for antibiotics. All she had was some nasal congestion. "Mommy, you can take your baby home today. She will be fine with some normal saline drops. She has no need for any antibiotics. "A sense of relief swept over me; I called Winston immediately and started preparing to take Gianna home.

I had no doubt what the enemy had tried but God delivered again. As we drove home, I gave God thanks for his faithfulness to us in every situation. I was holding my second miracle in my hands!

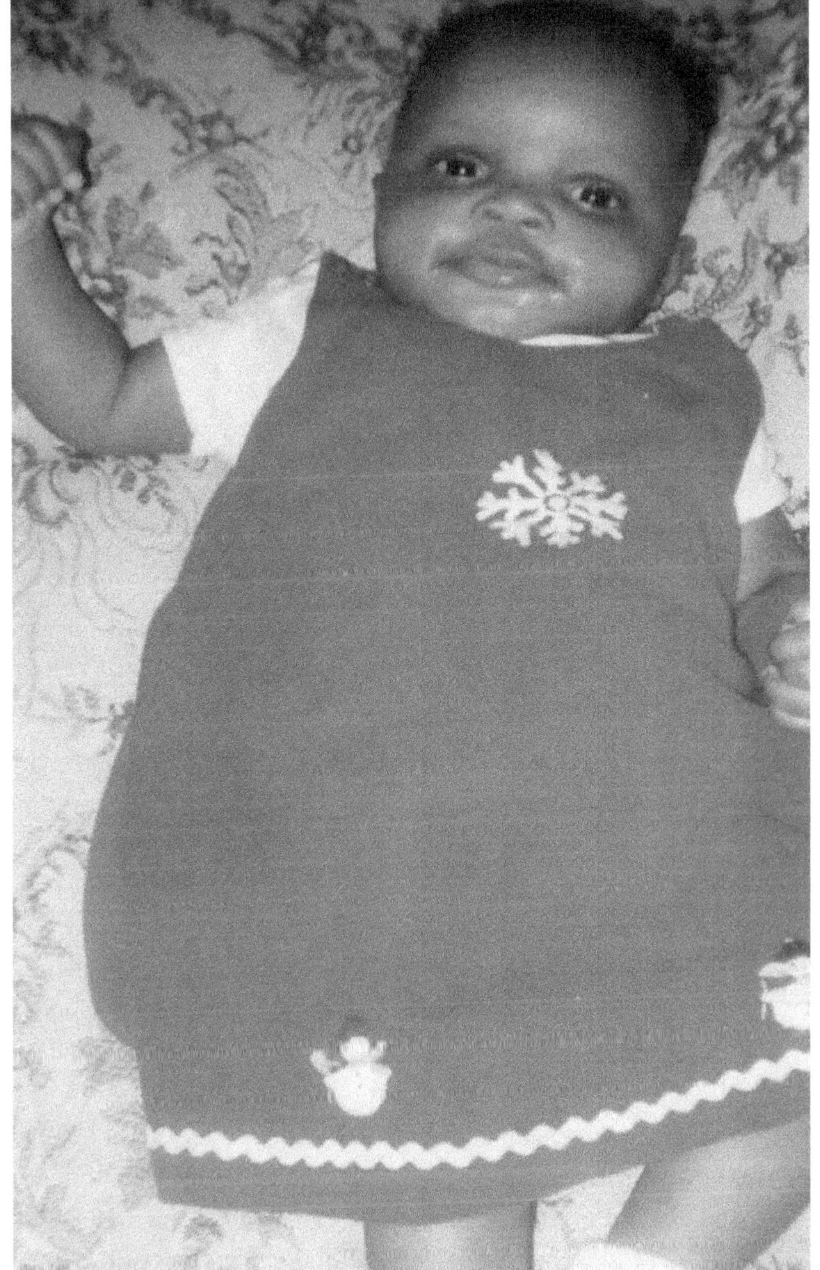

AND THEN THERE WERE THREE

The next three years went by quickly. Motherhood was fun: the two girls were very close and we captured the memories as time progressed. They were both now enrolled in Kindergarten and I had completed my training in Counselling Psychology and continued my job as a teacher. The adjustment to parenting was an ongoing process as each stage brought its own new experiences. What we were sure of was that God had turned a very trying period of our lives into a testimony.

"Megan, why are you eating snacks so often?" Cheryl asked. Cheryl was my closest friend at work. She knew me well and she noticed I was snacking a lot in between classes. "Me?" I replied. "I just feel peckish." "This is more than peckish. You are pregnant." She insisted. "What?! Are you crazy?" I asked her.

"Nope. I am not crazy. You are pregnant." She said confidently. I smiled and left the staff room for my next class but the conversation played in my head repeatedly like a scratched record. Over the next two weeks I realized I felt nauseous in the evenings and was certainly feeling hungry more often than usual. I said nothing to anyone about how I was feeling but deep down I began to believe that what my friend suspected was true.

Eventually I decided to purchase a pregnancy test to settle my mind and it was negative. I went to work the next day and told Cheryl she was wrong, I was not pregnant. The symptoms persisted and I started to wonder if something was wrong that needed to be addressed. I made an appointment to see Dr. Mitchell and I remember vividly the look on her face as she did her checks after I had recounted symptoms and the fact that I did a pregnancy test and it was negative. She had a very calm look and she sent me to the nurse to do another test and return to her office.

She asked me how the girls were doing while we waited for the nurse to return with the completed pregnancy kit. The door opened and as the nurse came in Dr Mitchell said, "Take it Megan and look at it. "

What I saw as I pulled the kit out of the wrapper left me speechless for a few seconds. There were two bright red lines- a new baby was on board! Dr. Mitchell smiled, I still believe she already knew. I was almost eight weeks pregnant. Wow. As soon as I stepped out of the office, I called Winston and gave him the news. He was excited. This sounded like the promise God had made - my womb was blessed. The mouth of the Lord had spoken and the manifestation continued. Needless to say, my friend Cheryl was over the moon with excitement as she now had evidence of what she suspected all along.

I knew the procedure. I would have to do a cerclage procedure at 14 weeks and I prepared for it and prayed that all would go well. I showed up at the hospital for the procedure. I had done this twice before but somehow I knew I had to be vigilant. I kept praying as I waited my turn. While waiting on the stretcher to go to the theatre a doctor came in took up my file called my name and said to the nurse, "She is the one for the D & C, right?" I quickly responded, "No doctor not me!" A D & C is a procedure done to clean a woman's uterus of any residue after a miscarriage. The devil is a liar! Immediately the nurse corrected him - "No doctor she is here for a cerclage her pregnancy is fine."

I gave God thanks as I realized that He was in the room. The enemy was still trying but God is always reigning. About 30 minutes later it was my turn and they wheeled me into the theatre. They explained the procedure and started administering the anesthetics. Strangely I could still hear the doctor and nurses speaking. The doctor started the procedure and although I was too sedated to speak, I could feel everything. It was excruciating but there was nothing I could do. This did not happen during the first two cerclage procedures. I then heard one of the nurses say, "Doctor her heart rate is increasing fast. We need to stop." The doctor told her she just wanted to finish. The pain was getting worse and I could hear the machine monitoring my heart-the sound kept going faster and faster, the nurse pleaded but the doctor seemed determined to continue. "Doctor, are you going to let this woman die on us! Stop!" the nurse shouted. The doctor stopped and the nurse suggested they give me more anesthetics once my heart rate went down. I could not speak but I was asking God for mercy on me and the child I was carrying.

I woke up sometime later in the recovery area. As I opened my eyes, I saw a nurse standing beside me checking my pulse rate.

"Are you a Christian? she asked. I was still very drowsy but I nodded and said yes. She said "God had me in that room for you today. You and your baby could have died in there." I told her I heard and felt everything and thanked her for what she had done. God had shown himself a very present help in trouble for me in that operation theatre. The weapon formed but it did not prosper!

The rest of the pregnancy was smooth and uneventful. My greatest challenge was having to work as a full-time teacher and travelling almost 20 miles to work and serving in my local church as a minister and counsellor throughout what was considered a high-risk pregnancy. But God watched over His word to perform it. My two first daughters were excited to know a baby was coming home soon and they enjoyed feeling the baby's movements on Mommy's tummy.

We learned we were having another baby girl and we prepared to welcome her. Due in December I was excited to have a daughter born in the same month as I was. My doctor's visit was a day after my birthday. I had my bag packed. As Dr Mitchell completed her regular checks she told me, "Megan, you will not be going home tonight you are actually in labour." I was sent to the labour ward but there was no further progress at all even until the next morning.

My pastor, mentors, family and friends were all checking in and some were in intense prayer. One particular minister called at approximately 9 a.m. in the morning. When I told him I was still waiting, he asked, "Are you ready?" I said yes. He said, "Are you sure?" Again, I said yes. He told me he was going back to pray again and the baby would be here very soon. Shortly after that Dr Mitchell came to see me and she too was surprised that I was not ready for delivery. She however encouraged me (as usual) and said the nurses would call her when I was ready.

About 3 minutes after Dr. Mitchell left, I felt a sharp pain and I literally felt the baby drop into my lower abdomen. I shouted, "Nurse, the baby is coming." The nurse closest to me laughed and commented, "That's not possible Mommy. Dr Mitchell just checked and you were just 6 cm dilated!" "Nurse, I am serious." After that she noticed I was pushing and came to check. She started moving frantically calling other nurses and getting me ready for the delivery room. I was fully dilated and baby Zari was making her entrance. I felt like I was in a movie as nurses rushed me on a stretcher begging me to breathe hard but not to push. At that point it was almost impossible to carry out those instructions as little Miss was doing her own pushing. Dr. Mitchell rushed into the room, threw her rings on the counter, washed her hands, put on her scrubs and with one last push from me my third miracle entered the world. She was beautiful-just like her sisters and I knew my heart had been captured all over again.

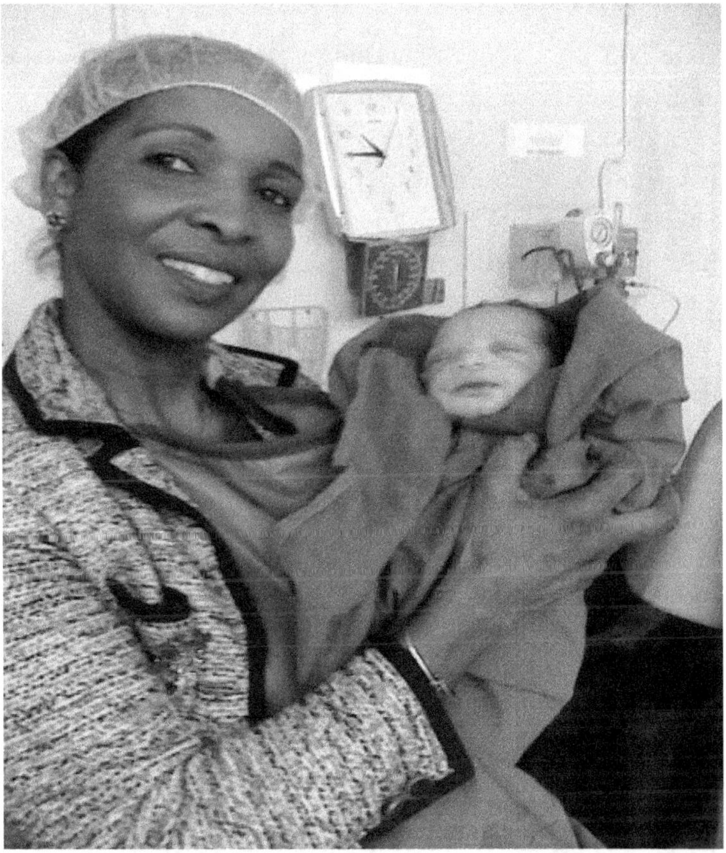

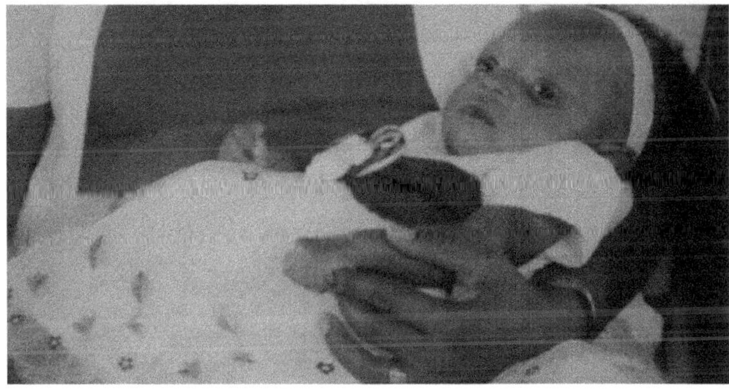

DEDICATING THEM TO GOD.

Based on the journey of waiting I felt the need to have a special dedication service for each of the girls instead of the traditional one done in a church service. As we had done for Abigail, her two younger sisters had their own dedication ceremony and celebration. Specially invited guests of friends and family who had in some way been a part of the journey were invited and the ceremonies were video recorded so the girls could watch it later on in life. The presence and power of God was evident in each ceremony in a unique way.

The ensuing years were filled with adventure and a good mix of challenges; (parenting is no joke!) but it has certainly been a journey of joy, testimonies and memories. Adjusting to parenting two toddlers and a baby was a whole new experience but Winston and I understood the mercy that had enveloped us and we were determined to show our gratitude to God by parenting well. We had never walked this road before so where we needed help, we reached out for it. We embraced the assignment and were invested in honouring God by doing our best and yielding our imperfections to him. There are no perfect parents but there are great ones-the latter was our aim.

Grace had been multiplied. For ten years I had waited and in 5 years God blessed us with three children. Fifteen years had passed and we were experiencing triple grace. What the mouth of the Lord had spoken, his hands had certainly performed. It is the Lord's doing and it is marvelous in our eyes.

Chapter 10

LIVING THE PROMISE - RAISING THE PROMISED SEED

TRIPLE FOR MY TROUBLE

God has a way of answering prayers in a language that leaves you speechless. After ten long years of waiting, after the tears, the tests, the unexplained losses, the disappointments, the prophecies, the prayers and the declarations, He answered. Not once, but three times. I never imagined that I would deliver three beautiful daughters in five years. Three miracles that shifted my story from tragedy to triumph. My life had changed. God had kept his promise of being my glory and the lifter of my head. I was no longer a woman wearing shame; I was a living testimony.

There are days I still walk through my house and feel awe, whispering to myself, "Look what the Lord has done." or thinking, "Is this really me?" For so long all I had were prayers, dreams, and the hope that maybe one day I would hold in my arms, a child of my own. The silence that once echoed through my home was replaced by crying newborns, squealing toddlers, and the laughter of little girls running across floors and playing happily in the yard I once paced in prayer and tears. Today I enjoy meaningful conversations, growing moments and joy that remind me of just how much God has blessed me.

Motherhood found me-divinely, loudly and beautifully: and it came in a way that only God could have orchestrated. He created a journey and wrote a story from my life-all for His glory. Each pregnancy felt like stepping into a fresh miracle—precious, unexpected, and deeply personal. Each journey was different, and each child, unique.

My first daughter, Abigail, is my message of hope and trust made tangible. She arrived like sunshine after a long bleak storm, teaching me that God still remembers; that he hears and answers prayer (Her middle name means God has answered our prayers). We know it was the Lord's doing and it was marvellous in our eyes: that became the theme for her dedication ceremony. Abigail has taught me that waiting is never wasted and delay does not always mean denial. Interestingly, she is very selective in what she allows to fluster her -she remains calm even in some situations that look daunting- as if she is saying "Calm down people-it will work out!" Although as a toddler, she was very quiet, as she grew, her wisdom, courage and resilience began to manifest. Her first love was and continues to be dancing. But what I have realized over the years is that the same way her birth gave us hope, she continues to have that same impact on her friends and peers. They speak openly about how conversations with her leave them feeling encouraged and hopeful even on their lowest days. Isn't God amazing?!

My second daughter reflects abundance and grace- God's bold proclamation: *"I am the God who does exceedingly, abundantly above all you can ask or think."* Through her birth, he showed me that he has a limitless supply and can easily exceed my expectations. He had been gracious to us – and she was named Gianna-a gracious gift from God. She is a constant reminder that God blesses abundantly and often when we least expect. He does not just restore; He multiplies and he does it swiftly and boldly for the glory of his name.

Gianna is the 'go hard or go home' child and seems to carry an indomitable drive to maximize the gift of life and to enjoy every moment of it. As I held her and prayed in the first few days of her life, I sensed she would be making big moves in life. Her dedication theme was "Look Out World-Here I Come." Little did I know how prophetic that statement was! At just 5 years old she was named MVP for her Kindergarten track team and at 10 years old she became a published author and was subsequently interviewed on national radio and television and featured in The Gleaner newspaper. She carries an inner drive that is contagious and that doesn't allow her to settle. Once she conceives something in her heart, she has an unshakable belief that it is achievable, and she will pursue it relentlessly. This drive is what resulted in her first book: *"Learn to Use Your Wings."* We give Jesus all the glory as her journey continues to unfold.

As mentioned earlier, even though I wanted a third child I had no clue I was pregnant for a while. My third blessing reflects the strength and faithfulness of God- a reminder that when God restores, He does so in full measure. She carries a quiet yet profound strength. I call her my gentle giant; she has a peace that is hard to explain but impossible to ignore.

During my pregnancy with her, I had the sweetest times of personal praise and worship. I had always loved music but during those nine months, music and worship took on a whole new meaning for me. Even as I drew closer to delivery, the Lord gave me a song related to His faithfulness and, as I lay in pain on the labour ward a few days later, I heard that same song being played on the radio as if God was reminding me that he was there. Her name, Zamariah, comes from the Hebrew word 'Zamar' which means instrument of praise. At just 3 years old she was dancing with her sisters in a Praise Academy of Dance production in Kingston, Jamaica. Tears welled in my eyes as I recalled years earlier when I sat in a similar concert, childless - and as I watched I whispered a prayer to the Lord- 'Lord if you bless me with girls I would love for them to dance with Praise Academy of Dance.' Here I was watching them on stage dancing for the glory of Jesus-another prayer answered.

The fact is, I didn't just get the child I prayed for; I received the children God predestined for me; and each of them was uniquely designed and pre-packaged with divine purpose. To this day I feel deeply encouraged and thankful when I look at each of them. They are messages from God in the flesh. Messages of hope, abundance and the faithfulness of God. Messages that announce God's sovereignty in the affairs of men.

Recently while speaking at an event, I referred to them as Miracle Signs and Wonders. I said it jokingly at the time, but in retrospect I understand how much it makes sense. My first daughter was the first of three miracles indeed. It was a sign and a shock to many that I had my second daughter and when the third came - many were in awe - in wonder at what the Lord had done for me. So yes, I have miracles, signs and wonders around me every day. Triple for my trouble, reminders that with God absolutely nothing is impossible.

MOTHERHOOD AFTER INFERTILITY: THE HIDDEN EMOTIONS

People saw the miracles, but they didn't see the shadows that lingered after years of barrenness and brokenness. Being blessed does not erase the imprint of where you've been. The journey to motherhood had left scars on my soul that the enemy would try to use to cause me to miss out on the joys of the blessing I received.

In the early days of raising my children, I carried an unspoken fear: fear that something would go wrong; fear that God might take back what He had given; fear that I wasn't doing enough. I worried about the girls especially when I was not with them and more so when they began attending school. The word of God says in 1 Timothy 4 vs. 7, *"God has not given us a spirit of fear but of power, love and a sound mind."* I had to keep repeating that scripture and believing God to deliver me from the crippling thoughts that fear produced.

Infertility had taught me to brace myself for disappointment. Motherhood was teaching me to exhale, to trust God, to live fully in the promise without waiting for it to vanish. My emotional healing didn't happen instantly. It unfolded slowly through meditation on God's Word, whispered prayers over sleeping babies, bold declarations and moments when I realized I was no longer the woman begging for a miracle—I was the woman living in one.

I had to trust God with them. The truth is you and I cannot protect our children from everything, and we cannot always be with them. But the God who gave them to us is more than able to shield, cover and guide them always. Our weapon is prayer and God does the rest. Mothers must pray, we must operate in wisdom and be sensitive to the promptings of the Holy Spirit but it is God who ultimately preserves our children.

I recall one day when Abigail was in Kindergarten 1, I was resting at home and dozed off; I saw her crying at school-she looked scared and I suddenly awoke knowing something was wrong. I immediately prayed then called one of her teachers directly. She seemed surprised at the call but told me that Abigail was okay now and that she would explain later. I learned later that the older teacher was having a bad day and out of frustration had shouted at Abigail regarding something and hit her desk hard with a ruler. Abigail sat frozen for a while and was crying. The younger teacher had taken her up and placed her in her lap just before I got the vision and called. She assured me not to worry as she would keep an eye out for her for the rest of the school year which was almost over. Although my other daughters later attended the same school, that older teacher never got the opportunity to teach any of them- I would not have it.

MANAGING MOTHERHOOD: THREE GIRLS UNDER FIVE

Raising three daughters so close in age was its own adventure. My friend Deslyn, having experienced it firsthand, had warned me that it was no easy ride. Some days felt like a joyful whirlwind; others felt like organized chaos, but chaos wrapped in grace. There were baby bottles everywhere, mismatched socks, sudden meltdowns, cuddles, giggles, and the sacred exhaustion only mothers understand. But there was also a rhythm — a divine choreography — shaping us all. Each daughter added her own melody to the home.

They are older now, but the melody evolves and remains. Together, they create a symphony of life that reminds me daily that God restores in ways that take your breath away, stretch your heart and propel you into praise. Every day is a day of gratitude even the days when there is a lot going on and a lot to navigate: Parent Teacher meetings, assignments, birthdays, outings, family time, sibling disagreements, church-managing learning at 3 different levels and three different schools. One thing is certain, I continue to be deliberate about being fully present in their lives and celebrating milestones and the big and small moments. I am intentional about reminding them that they are gifts from God and that He is with them always to provide strength, grace and peace.

PARENTING THE PROMISED SEED

For me, embracing motherhood required growth. It demanded patience. It humbled me, refined me, and made me more dependent on God than ever before. It is not about perfection, it is about His grace sustaining me moment by moment and me learning that as a mother, I am a steward over three children whose true owner is God. My responsibility therefore is to stay connected to Him so that He can lead me in shepherding and nurturing all he has placed inside them. I knew their lives carried purpose long before I held them. I am raising promised seed and my actions must be intentional, deliberate and Holy Spirit led. Psalm 127 vs 3 states that children are the heritage of the Lord and the fruit of the womb is his reward. In Jeremiah 1 vs 5 God said to Jeremiah, Before I formed you in the belly, I knew you and before you came forth, I ordained you a prophet to the nations.

As you read this, I pray that revelation will hit your heart - children are not just born, they are sent. Within them lies a divine blueprint of who God intends for them to be and the impact they are to make in the earth. Your role as a parent is critical in the fulfillment of divine destiny. This cannot be taken lightly.

Pray for your children, even before they are conceived; pray over them in the womb; pray over them during infancy, childhood and adulthood. Pray over them; it is not an option. Your prayers and declarations help to shape their destiny and keep them in alignment with God's divine plan: *"Lord, let them be arrows in Your hand. Let them walk boldly in their identity. Let them know who they are and whose they are."*

Make worship, scriptures and declarations become a part of your home's atmosphere. Speak life into them even before they understand the words. Raising miracle children doesn't mean raising perfect children. It means stewarding their hearts, guiding their steps, and creating an environment where purpose can flourish. Children are gifts from God to us, but ultimately, they belong to Him.

FINDING GRATITUDE IN THE ORDINARY

Some of the most miraculous moments of motherhood are hidden in the ordinary:

- The tiny hands reaching for mine.
- The spontaneous hugs.
- The whispered "I love you Mommy."
- The milestones nobody else sees.
- The glass of water just because I look drained.
- The embraces and stories at the end of each school day,
- The simple family get-aways.
- The moments alone with each daughter.
- The birthdays, graduations, track meets, matches and performances.

After ten years of longing, I promised myself I would notice the small things. I would celebrate the ordinary; I would honour the God who turned my silent suffering and public shame, into a joyful celebration. Even on the hard days, gratitude has been my anchor. It keeps me grounded in the truth that this life — these girls — are a divine gift. Gratitude reminds me that what I went through was really not about me; it was about God and the people He would reach through my testimony.

BREAKING CYCLES, BUILDING LEGACIES

My parenting journey is not only about raising daughters, it is about rewriting history. Winston and I are determined by the grace of God, to break generational cycles of fear, disappointment and lack. We want our daughters to know love deeply, to feel safe, to grow with confidence, and to walk in the fullness of who God created them to be. We want them to inherit faith, not trauma; identity, not insecurity; purpose, not confusion.

LESSONS LEARNED WHILE LIVING THE PROMISE

- **Waiting is never wasted.**

Hope can be delayed but still delivered.

- **God doesn't just restore, He multiplies.**

True restoration comes with more than what was initially lost.

- **God finishes what He starts.**

Faithfulness is His nature.

- **Parenting is not just a role; it is a calling.**

A sacred assignment. A daily invitation to love, guide, nurture, and trust.

- **Parenting is journey of growing and learning.**

Parenting gives us the opportunity to plant seeds that will bear fruit long after we are gone. It carries within it, generational impact. It allows us to build a legacy rooted in prayer, resilience, and the unshakeable truth that God keeps His promises. He is a covenant keeping God.

Chapter 11

WHILE YOU WAIT...

"If the battle is won in the mind; the battle is won in the life."
(Apostle Dr. Courtney McLean)

The mind is the greatest place of warfare because it is the centre from which we process, navigate and respond to life and all that comes with it. What we believe ultimately affects what we do. Proverbs 23:7 states. *"As a man thinketh in his heart, so is he..."* As I reflect on my ten years of waiting, it is clear to me that our mindset and the posture we take while we wait for the manifestation of a promise can affect how long we wait. The battle must first be won in the mind and then it will manifest in life.

There are three types of people who wait: anxious waiters, passive waiters and active waiters. I will use the analogy of a busy international airport where several flights are delayed to describe who these people are and how they operate. The anxious waiters are the ones who go to the airline information desk regularly or check their airline app every two minutes to see the status of their flight. They may become irate because in spite of the reason for the delays, they need to leave. Their anxiety robs them of the ability to reason and even if there is a pending storm they just want to leave.

Passive waiters are people who, although experiencing delay, seem to have no care in the world and while waiting, they may get lost in their phones, start touring the airport or even fall asleep. They may

157

get so drawn into the distractions around them, they forget that they are awaiting the announcement of a flight! They may miss their flight!

Active waiters have a different posture than the first two. They may be seen working on their laptop in the airport, calling family or friends to update them, reading a book or making friends with other people around them but they are keeping a keen ear for the announcement of their flight, and they are ready to go when that comes.

What kind of 'waiter' are you in the context of waiting for the blessing of having a child? The anxious waiter is one who while praying and waiting is becoming impatient and angry with God and may even leave the faith because they think it is just not 'working' for them. Anxious waiters eventually begin to question God's word and may seek other means of having a child that may not be God's perfect will for them. Sarah was an anxious waiter when she offered her maid Hagar to Abraham to bear him children and she eventually lived to regret it. Modern medicine has provided options for couples who are having difficulty conceiving and we give God thanks for that -that may be the way God chooses to deliver your blessing but do not rush into anything unless you are led by God into it. Some couples experience infidelity while they wait because the anxious partner may succumb to the enemy's lies and goes outside of the marriage in a quest to have a child.

The passive waiter is one who knows they want a child but fails to really pursue its manifestation. Not much intentionality is evident; little or no effort is made to lay hold on the promises of God. Instead, they get consumed with things in life that are not as painful as facing the reality of their infertility. This is a feasible coping mechanism but the danger is that the passive waiters may miss the time of their visitation or miss divine instructions from God that could change their story for good. They have a 'Que Sera Sera' attitude-whatever will be will be; but the truth is we must contend for the promises that God has given to us.

The active waiter is one who is fully persuaded that God is able to do what seems impossible but understands that the blessing they are waiting for needs their co-operation for manifestation. For this kind of waiter, life doesn't stand still but neither does life consume them. Through strategic actions: prayers, giving, sowing seed, declarations and prophetic acts, the active waiter seeds his prophetic cloud until it bursts - giving birth to the promise he/she was waiting for. How does one seed their cloud? Through praying the word, declaring the word, believing the word, doing prophetic acts as led by the Holy Spirit, fasting and giving. Sometimes while you are waiting on your promised child you have to be a blessing to someone else's.

God seeks our cooperation and agreement when he wants to bless us with something mega. He waited for Mary's surrender and declaration: *"Be it unto me according to your word"* (Luke 1:38). He silenced Zechariah until John the Baptist was born because his unbelieving heart would have caused him to contaminate the seed of the promised forerunner of Christ whom his wife was to carry, with his faithless words (Luke 1: 20). The man or woman actively waiting for a promised child understands the power of intentionally coming in agreement and alignment with the will of God for their life.

I encourage you to seek to be an active intentional believer as you wait and contend for the promises of God to you. Waiting actively means fighting from a place of rest - knowing the outcome but realizing there is resistance from the enemy and you must push back. Ecclesiastes 11: 3 says *"If the clouds be full of rain, they empty themselves upon the earth…"* As you position yourself to seed your cloud be intentional about the following:

1.   The Power of the Spoken Word of God

Hebrews 4 vs. 12: *"For the word of God is quick, and powerful, and sharper than any two-edged sword, piercing even to the dividing asunder of soul and spirit, and of the joints and marrow, and is a discerner of the thoughts and intents of the heart."*

➢   God's Word Activates Faith

The Word of God carries power. It is God - breathed; it is spirit and it is life. In order to access the prophetic promises of God spoken over our lives; in order to see the manifestation of what you are praying for, you must find that word and begin to turn it into prayer, speaking it until it enters your heart and you believe it. You must be intentional about going into the Word and finding His promises relevant to your situation and activate those promises through your mouth!

As my pastor would say, Faith begins in your mouth. What does that mean? Romans 10:17 declares, *"So then faith comes by hearing, and hearing by the word of God."* Before your faith can develop you must hear. What should you hear? The word of God. Faith begins in the mouth. Begin to speak God's word over your life. Turn the word into prayer. Confess the word daily and watch your faith go to the next level. The spoken word of God has supernatural creative power. May you believe that it is living and active. Speak that word!!!!

Timothy 3: 16-17- *"All Scripture is God-breathed and is useful for teaching, rebuking, correcting and training in righteousness, so that the servant of God may be thoroughly equipped for every good work."*

➤ God's Word Mobilizes His angels

Psalm 103: 20- *"Bless the Lord, ye His angels, that excel in strength, that do His commandments, hearkening unto the voice of his word."* Understand that when you stand in your position as a covenanted son or daughter of God and speak his word, angels respond to carry out what is spoken. The Bible did not say they hearken to His word - specifically it says they hearken to the voice of His word. Who will give voice to the word of God in your life? God is not coming down to speak that word that He already released. You must now give voice to it and angels will respond.

➤ God's Word Guards the Mind

Psalm 119: 165- *"Great peace have they which love thy law: and nothing shall offend them."* (King James Version)

"Those who love Your law have great peace; Nothing makes them stumble. (Amplified Version)

When you feed on God's word, reading and meditating on it, the law of displacement begins to take place. God's truth begins to displace the lies and fears that were sown in your mind by your experiences in life. Eventually your mind becomes guarded by the Sword of the Spirit which is the Word of God (Ephesians 6: 17). Discouragement may come but it will find no place to dwell in you because you are guarded by His Word.

➢ God's Word Brings Forth Fruit

One of my favourite verses in the Bible (I have many) is the bold declaration God makes in Isaiah 55: 11, *"So shall my word be that goeth forth out of my mouth: it shall not return unto me void, but it shall accomplish that which I please, and it shall prosper in the thing whereto I sent it."* (K J V)

"So will My word be which goes out of My mouth; It will not return to Me void (useless, without result), Without accomplishing what I desire, and without succeeding in the matter for which I sent it." (Amplified Version)

God's word in your life will bear fruit. Believe that and develop an expectation for it. Miracles manifest in an atmosphere of expectation. May His word bear fruit in your life. May you testify! May it accomplish His will in you. May you testify!

2. The Power of Vision

Jeremiah 1: 11 "The word of the LORD came to me: 'What do you see, Jeremiah?' 'I see the branch of an almond tree,' I replied."

This conversation took place at the beginning of the prophet, Jeremiah's ministry. He needed to be focused on divine perspective rather than physical circumstances. It is important that as you wait for your blessing your vision is aligned with what God has in store for you. May you begin to see the righteous seed God has for you. May your vision line up with the future God has for you in the all-powerful name of Jesus!

3. The Eagle's Mindset-Climb!

Isaiah 40 :31 "But those who hope in the Lord will renew their strength. They will soar on wings like eagles; they will run and not grow weary, they will walk and not be faint."

I have always been intrigued by the eagle. There is much to be learned from this king of the birds. One thing that stands out about the eagle is its battle strategies. Eagles tend to fly alone and crows often seek to attack them by picking at them while in flight. The eagle usually doesn't react to the annoyance of the crow's persistence by fighting back. It simply increases its altitude. it climbs, because the crow cannot survive at a certain altitude in the air. As it elevates, the crow will die or be forced to let it go.

Waiting is warfare and as you wait, understand that your enemy, the devil goes about seeking to devour you. He will send attacks against your mind, your life and your faith. Hope in God and you will be strengthened. You must seek to continually level up in God. Do not settle. Each time the warfare intensifies you intensify your prayer, worship and intake of the Word of God. The victory is found in hiding in God. Do not be distracted by the devices of the enemy, he cannot survive in the oil and glory of God's presence. It's time to climb!

4. Don't Mingle Your Seed

Leviticus 19:19 — *"You shall not sow your field with mixed seed…"*

'Seed' here represents your faith and the positive declarations you have made about what you are expecting God to do. When we utter words of confessions that are contrary to what we are believing for, we are mingling the seed. In Leviticus chapter 19 verse 19, God instructed the Jews regarding their farming practices. He said, *"You shall not sow your field with mixed seed…"* The principle behind this command is very relevant to those who are waiting in faith. We must not mix or mingle our faith with fear, doubt and unbelief, it can affect the outcome. Proverbs 18 vs. 21 states, *"Death and life are in the power of the tongue: and they that love it shall eat the fruit thereof."* Be careful not to destroy your good seed; Practise coming into agreement with God with your words. Mingling seed means by your words and confessions you are sowing enemy seeds and mixing it with your faith. Don't use your own words to destroy what you are trying to build.

What does this look like in practice? At the point where my faith had developed to a certain level, I would speak to my body and say words like, "You will carry healthy children" or I would look in the mirror and speak to myself: "You will be the happy mother of children" or "One day soon I will be a mother". At times these words had to be spoken during my pregnancies when I was having discomforts that felt too similar to the miscarriages I had gone through, and the enemy would suggest thoughts that maybe it was happening again. I could not afford to mingle my seed. Even though I was thinking it, I refused to confirm it with my words. I spoke what I was believing for. Remember your words matter-you are likely to have what you say! Don't mingle your seed.

5. Do Not Get Weary: Stay Planted Under Pressure.

Galatians 6: 9 *"Let us not become weary in doing good, for at the proper time we will reap a harvest if we do not give up."*

Waiting can weary you. As the Bible says in Proverbs 13:12, *"Hope deferred makes the heart sick, but a longing fulfilled is a tree of life."* I can recall times on my journey to motherhood when I felt weary, battle worn, tired of the fight. It was in those moments when my will power and determination were most needed to get me back on my feet. A weary warrior is a potentially fallen warrior and so the enemy is always seeking to wear you out! Sometimes, the weary soldier on the battlefield has to find something within him that is greater than just his physical strength to keep him going. You must develop inner fortitude and tenacity leaning on God for strength to keep you from losing hope while you wait. At other times, the weary soldier must be helped by a soldier who is stronger than he is in that moment, who can help him to endure the battle and come out alive. May God send the right persons to stand with you in faith when you start to feel weary. As He did for me, may He cause your faith boosters to locate you right on time.

Paul encourages the believers in Galatians 6:9, not to get weary in well-doing because at the 'proper time' they would reap a harvest. That 'proper time' can also be called God's time. God has a set time to favour you but getting weary and inconsistent can delay that set time. I pray that you will not get weary and that weariness will never cripple or derail your faith. He who promised you is faithful. Whenever you feel weary remind yourself of the promises in God's word-boost your faith. Remember as you contend for what is rightfully yours - giving up is not an option

6. Let Nothing Move You

1 Corinthians 15:58 *"Therefore, my beloved brothers and sisters, be steadfast, immovable, always excelling in the work of the Lord…"*

This entire book is about learning to believe God until your faith produces fruit. The journey as you have seen was not easy for me but it shows that God is sovereign and merciful and He rules in the affairs of men. There were several times on the journey when I grappled with the 'What If' questions: "What if I had another miscarriage?" "What if something is wrong with the baby at birth?" "What if I never have a child?". You may be having these thoughts while you wait. The truth is any blessing we receive is on the account of God's decision to bless us. If he doesn't bless us with what we desire or in the way we desire, does that take away from His sovereignty, or does it prove it?

Philippians 4: 6 says *"Do not **be anxious** about anything, but in every situation, by prayer and petition, with thanksgiving, present your requests to God."* The posture of the heart while waiting must be one of unwavering loyalty to God and peace in Him. Recently Apostle Dr. Courtney McLean said these words during a sermon, which I find to be very powerful: "If you don't get the miracle, don't abort the destiny." We continue to love and serve God and fulfill purpose while we wait. Even when things are not going the way we want them to, because He is God, we trust His sovereignty, because we know Him as Father, we trust His love towards us; because of His faithfulness we live by faith and die in faith. In obedience to God's word we let nothing move us by doing the following:

➢ Trust His Sovereignty

"The Lord has established His throne in the heavens, And His sovereignty rules over all [the universe]." (Psalm 103: 19-Amplified Version). God is in control. We pray, we believe and know He can do all things and we stand in faith, but we trust His sovereignty. It means we have settled it in our hearts that He knows what we need, when we need it and how we need it. When Jesus taught His disciples to pray in Matthew Chapter 6, he started and ended His model prayer by acknowledging the Sovereignty of His Heavenly Father.

Matthew 6:9-10: *"Our Father, who is in heaven, Hallowed be Your name. Your kingdom come, Your will be done, On earth as it is in heaven."* Matthew 6:13: *"For Yours is the kingdom and the power and the glory forever. Amen."* God is sovereign over all. While we wait on the miracles, we yield to His sovereignty.

➢   Rest in His Love

Romans 8: 35, 37-39

*[35] **Who** shall separate us from the love of Christ? shall tribulation, or distress, or persecution, or famine, or nakedness, or peril, or sword? [37] Nay, in all these things we are more than conquerors through Him that loved us. [38] For I am persuaded, that neither death, nor life, nor angels, nor principalities, nor powers, nor things present, nor things to come, [39] Nor height, nor depth, nor any other creature, shall be able to separate us from the love of God, which is in Christ Jesus our Lord."*

It is interesting to note that Paul did not ask **what** can separate us from the love of God, but **"who"**; then he lists things not people: tribulation, distress, persecution, famine, nakedness, peril or sword. WOW-not what but who? Could these things be spirits sent by the enemy but masked as things and experiences happenings? May our eyes be opened to the enemy behind things. But remember Paul's point is that these things cannot separate us from God's love. In these things we are more than conquerors through Jesus who loved us. The conquering comes through the revelation of His love for us. God loves you and He will do nothing to hurt you. Be persuaded as Paul was that nothing can separate you from God's love. While you wait, may you find peace and rest in His love.

> ➤ Stand on His Faithfulness

God's faithfulness or what I call his track-record is a sure source of reassurance in the face of a reality that contradicts what you are expecting. The faithfulness of God is a theme that runs throughout the pages of the Bible:

- **2 Timothy 2:13 (ESV):** "If we are faithless, *he remains faithful*—for he cannot deny Himself."

- **Hebrews 10:23 (NIV):** "...for *He who promised is faithful.*"

- **Deuteronomy 7:9 (NIV):** "Know therefore that the Lord your God is God; *He is the faithful God*, keeping his covenant of love..."

- **Psalm 33:4 (NIV):** "For the word of the Lord is right and true; *He is faithful in all he does.*"

When we focus on God's faithfulness it will help us to stand in faith. If you have a miscarriage, if your baby has a health challenge, if you are increasing in age and still don't have a child - rest on God's track-record: He's got you! He is a covenant keeping God and even in the messiness of life because you are in covenant with Him-ALL things work together for good to you because you love Him and you are called according to His purpose.

Make a decision to believe that God is able to do what looks impossible. From now until the moment that you take your last breath, believe that you will see the goodness of God in the land of the living. David testified in Psalm 27: 13-14: *"I would have (fainted) lost heart, unless I had believed* that I *would see the goodness of the Lord in the land of the living.*[14] *Wait on the Lord; Be of good courage, And He shall strengthen your heart; Wait, I say, on the Lord!"* The repellent for fainting is faith-have confidence in God. Wait in confidence.

I end this chapter with a reflection from the Word on some stalwarts of faith from Hebrews Chapter 11: 11-13: *"**And by faith even Sarah, who was past childbearing age, was enabled to bear children because she considered Him faithful who had made the promise.** ¹²And so from this one man, and he as good as dead, came descendants as numerous as the stars in the sky and as countless as the sand on the seashore.¹³ **All these people were still living by faith when they died.** They did not receive the things promised; they only saw them and welcomed them from a distance, admitting that they were foreigners and strangers on earth."*

The King James Version of the Bible says, *"These all died in faith…"* (vs. 13). May you still be living in faith when you die. Consider him faithful who has promised and be enabled to experience His supernatural power in your life. While you wait, create an atmosphere of standing in faith on the living active word of God, for the just shall live by faith. There is no other way.

Chapter 12

PRAYERS AND DECLARATIONS

"A closed mouth is a closed destiny."
-Apostle Dr. Courtney McLean

Mark 11: 22-24- *"22 So Jesus answered and said to them, "Have faith in God. 23 For assuredly, I say to you, whoever says to this mountain, 'Be removed and be cast into the sea,' and does not doubt in his heart, but believes that those things he says will be done, he will have whatever he says. 24 Therefore I say to you, whatever things you ask when you pray, believe that you receive them, and you will have them."*

Prophetic prayers and declarations are prayers and bold announcements that are spoken in agreement and based on the Word of God and His promises. The secret to answered prayer is praying the Word. God is not moved by simple emotions; He responds to faith in His Word. His angels hearken unto the voice of His Word. In Mark 11 verses 22-24 (shared above) Jesus told his disciples that for those who believe they will have whatever they say.

As disciples of Christ and sons of God, we must develop the habit of putting feet to our faith though prophetic prayers and declarations. It is also imperative to understand the power of having Jesus in our lives. He is our very present help. A very popular story from His time on earth is the one found in Mark 4 verse 35-41. Jesus had instructed his disciples to sail over to the other side of the lake and he went to the bottom of the boat to sleep. A storm rose while he was asleep and though the disciples had been walking with Jesus their faith level was still low. Fear gripped them and the seasoned men of the sea recognized their helplessness . Their lives were in danger but someone remembered that Jesus was in the boat! Although Jesus later rebuked them for lacking faith, he responded to their cry for help, rebuked the storm and saved them from disaster. Despite your knowledge and expertise, there is a power that is released when you recognize who your Help is. As a child of God, Jesus is in your boat. Don't confine Him to the bottom of the boat. Give Him access to all areas of your life! Call upon Him when you need Him. He promises to show up for you.

> - **Psalm 17:6:** *"I call on you, my God, for you will answer me; turn your ear to me and hear my prayer."*
> - **Psalm 50:15:** *"And call upon Me in the day of trouble; I will deliver you, and you shall glorify Me."*
> - **Psalm 18: 6:** *"In my distress I called upon the Lord; to my God I cried for help. From His temple He heard my voice, and my cry to Him reached His ears."*
> - **Jeremiah 33: 3:** *"Call unto me, and I will answer thee, and shew thee great and mighty things, which thou knowest not."*

Prayer is a conversation with God. Prophetic prayers and declarations help you to come in agreement with God based on His written or revealed truths. Use these prayers and declarations as a guide. Pour out your heart to God because He cares about you. Practice listening as a part of praying and be ready to write what you sense God saying to you. He promised to instruct you and guide you in the way you should go. Don't miss that! May your testimonies be mega!

PRAYER 1-THE BLESSING OF SONSHIP

Scripture: St. John 1: 12- *"But as many as received Him to them gave He power to become the sons of God."*

Prayer:

My Lord and my God, my blessed Heavenly Father. I thank you that because I have received Jesus, I am a son of God. Sons have rights. Sons have access. Sons have inheritance. I receive all that is rightfully mine. Healing, wholeness, fruitfulness. Nothing missing, nothing broken, nothing lacking. I thank you Father for the blessing of sonship in Jesus mighty name!

Declaration:

I am God's daughter. As His daughter it is my right to be healed and whole. Everything in my body comes in alignment now. My womb is blessed. I do not struggle to conceive. These are my rights as God's daughter. I claim what is mine and I walk in it daily in Jesus name. Amen!

PRAYER 2-BE FRUITFUL AND MULTIPLY

Scripture: Genesis 1: 28 *"And God blessed them, and God said unto them, Be fruitful, and multiply, and replenish the earth, and subdue it..."*

Prayer:

My Lord and my God my blessed Heavenly Father. I exalt You as the Creator and ruler of the Universe. Hallowed be Your name. By Your word I am blessed and commanded to be fruitful and multiply. I confess Your word over my body and in my life. I am fruitful. My husband and I are fruitful. According to the order of Genesis 1:28, I thank You that our reproductive systems are healed, blessed and fruitful. We carry and deliver healthy seed in the name of Jesus Christ, the Son of the Living God.

Declaration:

I receive the blessing of the Lord and declare fruitfulness over my life and my womb. Every delay, obstacle, and limitation is destroyed by the power of Almighty God. I stand in faith, hope, and expectation, trusting God to bring forth life according to His promise. Everything that is working against my fruitfulness, whether through my words, the words or actions of others, generational cycles - everything fighting against my fruitfulness be neutralized in Jesus mighty name! I am the blessed of the Lord. My seed will be mighty in the earth!

PRAYER 3-REMEMBERED BY GOD

Scripture: 1 Samuel 1:19 & 27: *"…and Elkanah knew Hannah his wife; and the Lord remembered her. [27] For this child I prayed; and the Lord hath given me my petition which I asked of Him.."*

Prayer:

My Blessed Heavenly Father I come to You in the name of Jesus. I thank You that You hear the cry of Your people, so I know that You hear my cry today. You said we should call unto You and You will answer and show us mighty things. I call unto You for the blessing of the womb. I call unto You for the blessing of children. Hear me O God like You heard Hannah and remember me as You remembered Hannah. The blood of Jesus speaks more excellent things for me. I am remembered. I am remembered! I give you praise O God that You have heard me and I prepare to hold the child I prayed for. I give you praise because You are faithful to Your promises and I receive by faith my request in Jesus mighty name! Amen.

Declaration:

I declare that the Lord remembers me. My tears are not forgotten, and my prayers are heard. I declare divine response to my prayers. What I have asked of the Lord, He is able to bring to pass. I declare that my petitions lifted in faith will meet God's ear and He will answer me. I stand in faith, not fear; I stand with an expectation, not doubt. I know that the God who remembered Hannah is mindful of me. I receive God's answer in His way and His time, and I give Him glory in advance. I walk in peace and joy knowing that my prayer is answered. I am remembered. Hallelujah!

PRAYER 4-SICKNESS IS TAKEN AWAY

Scripture: Exodus 23: 25 & 26: *"And ye shall serve the Lord your God, and He shall bless thy bread, and thy water; and I will take sickness away from the midst of* *thee.[26] There shall nothing cast their young, nor be barren, in thy land: the number of thy days I will fulfil."*

Prayer:

My Lord and my God, my blessed Heavenly Father by Your grace I serve the Lord Christ. Thank You that Your promises are yea and Amen. I stand on the promise of Exodus 23: 25-26, You bless my bread and my water, and You take sickness far from me. Sickness has no place in my body. I am the temple of the living God. Take sickness far away from me O God. Have mercy upon me and drive sickness far from me my Father. Every sickness in my bloodline be driven away now in Jesus mighty name. I will not cast my young, I carry my pregnancies to full-term- according to Your word. Barrenness is not my portion in Jesus' name! I thank You Father for the blessing of health, fertility and full-term thriving pregnancies in Jesus mighty name!

Declaration:

I declare that as I serve the Lord my God, His blessing rests upon my life. My bread is blessed, my water is blessed, and every source of provision is sanctified. I declare that sickness is taken away from my midst.

My body comes into divine order under the hand of God. I declare that there is no miscarriage, no barrenness, and no loss in my body and in my union. Life, strength, and fruitfulness prevail by the power of God. I declare the fulfillment of my days according to God's promise. I am whole, healed, and complete. I am preserved by the Word of God! Amen.

PRAYER 5-HE LIFTS MY HEAD

Scripture: Psalm 3: 3-4: *³ But thou, O Lord, art a shield for me; my glory, and the lifter up of mine head. ⁴ I cried unto the Lord with my voice, and He heard me out of His holy hill.*

Prayer:

My Lord and my God, my blessed Heavenly Father from the days of my conception You have been a shield for me. You saw me when I was being knitted together in my mother's womb. This day I call upon You O Lord. You are my shield my glory and You lift my head. Thank You that You are hearing me out of Your holy hill. My heart looks up to You because my help comes from You. Everything that has caused me to walk in shame is neutralized. You are the lifter of my head. Shield me from discouragement and shame. Shield me from fear and disappointment. You can change my story. Lift my head O God! Lift my head and show yourself strong on my behalf and cause me to testify. I give You thanks for hearing me in the all-powerful name of Jesus!

Declaration:

The Lord is my shield and my glory; He lifts my head above delay, disappointment, and fear. I declare that my head is not bowed by waiting. I am not defined by my waiting. I cry out to the Lord, and He hears me from His holy place. My prayers rise, my hope stands, and my faith remains steady. I trust the God who sees me, covers me, and carries my future. My story is held in His hands, and He will be glorified in it. He is my glory and the lifter of my head. Amen.

PRAYER 6 - A JOYFUL MOTHER OF CHILDREN

Scripture: Psalm 113:9: *"He maketh the barren woman to keep house, and to be a joyful mother of children. Praise ye the Lord."*

Prayer:

My Heavenly Father, I exalt you I honour and worship you mighty God. You do miracles so great. There is nothing impossible with You. I thank You in advance that my story is changing in my favour. I reject barrenness and I receive fruitfulness. I will be the joyful mother of children. Touch everything in my body and in my husband's body that opposes that truth. O Lord empower me to carry children. Empower us for parenthood. I give You praise for what You are doing in my life, for Your glory. In Jesus mighty name I pray, Amen.

Declaration:

I am a happy mother of children. ___________________ (Put your name in the blank space) will hold, nurse and raise children with joy for the glory of God. It is turning around for me.

PRAYER 7 - THE SET TIME TO FAVOUR ME HAS COME

Scripture: Psalm 102:13: *"You will arise and have mercy on Zion; For the time to favour her, Yes, the set time, has come."*

Prayer:

My Lord and my God, I thank You that You arise on behalf of Your people. I receive Your mercy and trust Your perfect timing. I believe that You are moving even now, aligning outcomes for my good. I rest assured that my life is not delayed but ordered because You promised to order my steps. I trust You O God, for favor, restoration, and fulfillment according to Your divine plan. Amen.

Declaration:

I declare that my set time of favour has come. Favour is released to me. God will arise and have mercy on ________________ (Put your name in the blank space) for the set time for her favour has come. Favour finds me, restoration follows me, and God's purpose unfolds in my life. I walk by faith, confident that God is at work and His timing is perfect. God is shifting men and positioning destiny helpers to show me high favour. The appointed time to favour me has come. I give You praise my Lord and King. Amen.

PRAYER 8 - IT SHALL TURN FOR A TESTIMONY

Scripture: Luke 21:13: *"And it shall turn to you for a testimony."*

Prayer:

My Lord and my God, my blessed Heavenly Father, I bring every trial, delay, and difficult season I face before You. What feels heavy to me is not hidden from You. I cast all my cares on You. I refuse to be anxious. I choose to trust you. Give me the grace to stand, the wisdom to know how to respond, and the faith to trust You fully. Use this season to reveal Your power, Your faithfulness, and Your glory through my life.

Faithful God, I thank You that nothing I walk through is wasted. I receive strength for this season and grace for every step. I declare that this moment will turn into a testimony of Your faithfulness.

What looks like delay will reveal Your glory. I stand confident in You, anchored in Your love and secure in Your promises. I move forward in faith, knowing that You are with me and You will bring me through. I receive by faith in Jesus' mighty name.

Declaration:

I declare that what I am walking through will become my testimony. This season will speak of God's faithfulness, not my defeat. I declare that pain will produce purpose, and delay will give way to destiny.

What the enemy meant to silence me, will amplify the work of God in my life. This will turn for a testimony. God is with me, strengthening me, bringing me through and changing my story for His glory.

PRAYER 9 -GOD IS WITH ME

Scripture: Deuteronomy 31:8 "The Lord himself goes before you and will be with you; he will never leave you nor forsake you. Do not be afraid; do not be discouraged."

Prayer:

My Heavenly Father, I thank You that You go before me and You are with me. I have no need to fear therefore I release every anxiety, fear and apprehension because I will never be forsaken by You. In spite of what I may be experiencing, discouragement fear and abandonment are far from me because You are with me and You will never leave. I have no need to fear because You are here.

Declaration:

I declare that the Lord goes before me and prepares my path. I am never alone; God is with me in every season. Fear has no power over my mind, my heart, or my future. I declare that I am strong and courageous through the strength of the Lord. I declare that I will not be discouraged, for God is always with me.

PRAYER 10: STEPPING INTO THE NEW THING

Scripture: Isaiah 43: 18-19: *"Remember ye not the former things, neither consider the things of old. Behold, I will do a new thing; now it shall spring forth; shall ye not know it? I will even make a way in the wilderness, and rivers in the desert."*

Prayer:

My Lord and my God, my blessed Heavenly Father, I thank You that You are the God of new beginnings. Today, I choose to release the former things—the disappointments, the delays, the wounds, the seasons that no longer serve Your purpose in my life. I let go of what was, so I can fully receive what is evolving. Lord, You declared in Isaiah 43:18 that You are doing a new thing. I open my heart to perceive it. Even when I cannot see clearly, I trust Your hand at work beneath the surface. Make a way for me where there seems to be no way. Create rivers in dry places, restore hope where weariness once lived, and bring life where things felt barren.

Give me discernment to recognize the doors You are opening and courage to walk through them without fear. Open my eyes to see divine connections. I yield to Your timing, Your will, and Your divine purpose. I choose to live in an attitude of expectation for my new thing in the mighty name of Jesus!

Declaration:

I declare that I am no longer bound to former things; my past does not define my present or my future. God is doing a new thing in my life, and I see it by faith. I declare that every dry place in my life is receiving fresh rivers from God. God is making a way for me where there seems to be no way. I step boldly into the new season, confident and unafraid.

AUTHOR'S WORD OF ENCOURAGEMENT

It has been such a blessing recounting this miraculous journey to unwavering faith. Each person's journey is unique but the common thread in each of our lives is that if we allow Him, God is working for our good and for His glory. If you are going through your wilderness experience, be encouraged, it won't always be like this. Your set time will come. Until then, don't lose heart and do not lose faith. God changed my story and He can change yours too. Jesus Christ is the same yesterday, today and forever (Hebrews 13:8). He has the final say.

If you have read this book, you got a first-class ticket into ten years of my life where God changed my story for His glory and you got a firsthand view of His unwavering love even in toughest times. If you have not yet accepted Jesus as your Saviour, I invite you to do so now. Ask Him to forgive you of all your sins and bring you into a personal walk with Him. That decision gives you the right to become God's legitimate son or daughter and gives you full access to a covenantal relationship with the Him.

If you are already a disciple of Jesus, may you come to a place of establishment in God where nothing can move you, where you know that nothing can separate you from the love of God. Stay close to Him as you navigate the seasons of life. If you are going through a wilderness experience, remember it shall turn for you into a testimony

I leave you with one of my favourite Bible verses:

"Now to him who is able to do immeasurably more than all we ask or imagine, according to his power that is at work within us, to him be glory in the church and in Christ Jesus throughout all generations, for ever and ever!" Ephesians 3: 20 (NIV)

Remember with God nothing shall be impossible! Shalom. Shalom.

"Hope deferred maketh the heart sick, but when the desire cometh, it is a tree of life!" -Proverbs 13:12

OTHER BOOKS BY THE AUTHOR

(Available on Amazon)

Directing Your Arrows: A Strategic Approach to Successful Parenting (2020)

To Love and To Hold: Vol. 1; Built To Last: 7 Foundational Principles for Success at Marriage (2023)

Teen Queen E.M.E.R.G.E Empowerment Journal (2024)